Rapt in colour

Korean textiles and costumes of the Chosŏn dynasty

조선시대의 한국의상과 보자기

Claire Roberts and Huh Dong-hwa (eds)

Powerhouse Museum, Sydney, Australia and The Museum of Korean Embroidery, Seoul, Korea

Australian edition first published 1998
Powerhouse Publishing, Sydney

Powerhouse Publishing
part of the Museum of Applied Arts and Sciences
PO Box K346 Haymarket NSW 1238 Australia
The Museum of Applied Arts and Sciences incorporates the Powerhouse Museum and Sydney Observatory.

Editors : Claire Roberts, curator of Asian decorative arts and design*,
and Huh Dong-hwa, director, The Museum of Korean Embroidery
Project management : Julie Donaldson* and Huh Dong-hwa
Copy editing : Julie Donaldson*
Design : Professor Kang Yoon-Sung, College of Fine Arts, Kyonggi University
Design Assistant : Youn Seung-Ho
Produced by : Phoenix Offset. Printed in China
Fonts : Univers Condensed and Futura Condensed

* Powerhouse Museum

National Library of Australia
Cataloguing-in-Publication
Roberts, Claire, 1959-
Rapt in colour : Korean textiles and costumes of the Chosŏn dynasty

Bibliography
ISBN 1 86317 074 X

1. Costume-Korea-History-Yi dynasty, 1392-1910
2. Textile design-Korea-History-Yi dynasty, 1392-1910
Ⅰ. Huh, Dong-hwa. Ⅱ. Title

391 009519

Published in conjunction with the exhibition of the same name at the Powerhouse Museum, Sydney, Australia, 10 September 1998 - 18 July 1999, Immigration Museum, Old Customs House , Melbourne,
10 October 1999 - 27 February 2000

Supported by

AUSTRALIA-KOREA FOUNDATION

THE MYER FOUNDATION

KOREAN AIR

Cover image : Yibul Po (wrapping cloth for bedding), line - patterned silk gauze (*sa*) decorated with patchwork design, 19th century, (112cm, 112cm).

C o n t e n t s

Foreword

It gives me great pleasure that the Powerhouse Museum is able to bring this inspiring collection of textiles from The Museum of Korean Embroidery in Seoul to Australia for the enjoyment of our community. This is the first significant Korean exhibition ever to come to Australia, and the first international travelling exhibition to be held in the Powerhouse Museum's Asian Gallery.

Through its exhibition and publication programme, the Powerhouse Museum is committed to making Asian cultures more accessible to Australian audiences. This exhibition is particularly appropriate given the extraordinary way in which these objects, by virtue of their unique and striking designs, are able to transcend their own time and place and appeal to our own aesthetic sensibility. At the same time the objects offer us a rich insight into Korean history, culture, customs and lifestyles.

I would like to thank Dr Huh Dong-hwa, Director of The Museum of Korean Embroidery who has made his collection available for display and has worked tirelessly to bring this exhibition to Australia, and the Korean Ministry of Culture and Tourism and the Korean Overseas Culture and Information Service for making that possible. I would also like to thank the exhibition sponsors for their support, notably the Australia-Korea Foundation, the Myer Foundation and Korean Air.

I would also like to express thanks to the museum staff who have worked on this project. In particular I wish to thank Claire Roberts, Curator of Asian decorative arts for initiating and co-ordinating this project and Min-Jung Kim, Assistant Curator, who has contributed an essay to this publication and provided invaluable Korean language liaison assistance.

Terence Measham
Director
Powerhouse Museum, Sydney, Australia

Foreword

I am delighted that this exhibition of costume and wrapping cloths focussing on the creativity of Korean women during the Chosŏn Dynasty will be held at the Powerhouse Museum in Sydney and in Melbourne in the lead up to the Olympic Games in 2000.

Traditional culture is relevant to the present and the future for when traditional culture meets the present it plays an important role in creating the future. Within any traditional culture there are elements that are unique and those that are shared with other cultures. When similarities or points of confluence are found between two cultures a higher degree of cross-cultural understanding is possible. The wrapping cloths in particular stand as a testimony to the creative talents of unknown Korean women. Each design is unique and of its time, yet many of the wrapping cloths also bring to mind images of modern abstract art. It is through their design that these objects can communicate with people from another culture across time. It is my sincere wish that this exhibition will contribute to the development of a greater understanding of Korean culture and Korean women's art.

In Korean literature needle work is often described as creativity borne of sorrow and regret. Seen from the perspective of the late twentieth century however these objects offer an insight into daily life and convey the will, hope and pleasure of creative women who lived during the Chosŏn dynasty. These women found happiness in needlework, a medium through which they could create a transcendent world full of life and humour, fuelled by their unlimited imagination.

This exhibition of costume and wrapping cloths from the Museum of Korean Embroidery in Seoul, provides visitors in Australia with an opportunity to experience the beauty of Korean textile traditions and to visualise the lives of the Korean women from days gone by.

I am grateful to the various individuals and organisations for their support of this exhibition. In particular I would like to thank Terence Measham, Director of the Powerhouse Museum, the Australia-Korea Foundation, the Myer Foundation, Korean Air, the Australian Embassy in Korea, the Korean Ministry of Culture and Tourism and the Korean Overseas Culture and Information Service, the Korean Embassy in Australia, and Claire Roberts and Min-Jung Kim of the Powerhouse Museum.

Huh Dong-hwa
Director
Museum of Korean Embroidery, Seoul, Korea

Acknowledgments

Many people have contributed to the preparation of this exhibition and publication. I would particularly like to thank Terence Measham, Director of the Powerhouse Museum for his support of this project and Dr Huh Dong-hwa Director of the Museum of Korean Embroidery in Seoul for his enthusiasm and support in bringing this exhibition to Australia. Thanks are also due to the Asian Art Musem of San Francisco, notably Dr Kumja Paik Kim, Curator of Korean Art for her pioneering work on the exhibition *Profusion of colour: Korean costumes and wrapping cloths of the Chosŏn dynasty,* which toured America 1995-96 and which forms the basis of this exhibition and publication, and to Dr Yi Sŏng-mi of the Academy of Korean Studies, Songnam-si, Korea, a contributing author.

In realising this exhibition in Australia sincere thanks are extended to Ki-Moon Baek (Consul-General, Republic of Korea), Moon-Sun Choi (Cultural Relations Officer, Australian Embassy, Seoul), Kyu Euk Chung (Consul, Consulate-General, Republic of Korea), Dr Young Yang Chung (USA), Carillo Gantner, Tony Hely (Ambassador, Australian Embassy, Seoul), Stephen Huang (Director, Australia-Korea Foundation), Clinton Jacka (Director of Public Affairs, Australian Embassy, Seoul), Professor Kang Yoon Sung (College of Fine Arts, Kyonggi University), Jung-Hoo Kim, Byong Hyon Kwon (former Ambassador, Republic of Korea), Lee Hyo-Jin, (Executive Officer, Australia-Korea Foundation, Seoul), Mrs San Lee (USA), Lee Yun Jung (Korea), Byung Kyu Min (former Consul-General, Republic of Korea), Moon Dong Suk (Ambassador, Republic of Korea) and Moon Kyung Sook, the Myer Foundation, Dr Young Sook Park (Sajeon House), Judith Rutherford (Events Coordinator, The Asian Arts Society of Australia), Song In-Sang (Curator, Seoul Arts Centre), Julie Steel (Ansett Australia), James Tigerman (USA) and Mack Williams (former Ambassador, Australian Embassy, Seoul).

Special thanks are also due to the many Powerhouse Museum staff who have contributed to this project in particular Jenny Cook (Corporate Development), Julie Donaldson (Powerhouse Publishing), Min-Jung Kim (assistant curator), Susan McMunn (exhibition coordinator) and Jisuk Han (exhibition designer).

Claire Roberts
Curator, Asian Decorative Arts & Design
Powerhouse Museum

Profusion of colour : Korean costumes and wrapping cloths of the Chosŏn dynasty

Kumja Paik Kim

From the earliest times in Korea taking care of silk worms, spinning thread, weaving cloth, sewing, and embroidery have been tasks assigned to women. The *Samguk sagi* (History of the Three Kingdoms Period) by Kim Pusik (1075-1151) mentions that during the reign of King Yuri (reign 24-57) the six districts were divided into two wards and that:

> the womenfolk of each group were led by a princess in a game. From the sixteenth day of the seventh month two sides gathered in the village courtyard every day to twist threads from early morning to the second watch. On the fifteenth day of the eighth month, the two teams were rated, and the losing team prepared wine and food to congratulate the winners ...[1]

Other stories suggest the high level of the development of sericulture, weaving, and the art of embroidery during the Three Kingdoms period (BC 57-AD 668). For example, commoners of the Silla Kingdom during King Soji's reign (479-500) are said to have worn colourful embroidered silk clothing. And Queen Chindok (reign 647-654), who initiated diplomatic relations with the Chinese Tang court, is said to have not only composed a poem titled *T'aep'yŏng song,* ('Ode to Peace') but to have it also embroidered on silk to present to the Tang emperor Taizong (reign 627-649).[2] That the production of fabrics and cutting, sewing, and embellishing clothes continued to be women's tasks throughout the history of Korea is well illustrated in genre paintings by Cho Yŏngsŏk (1686-1761) and Kim Hongdo (1745-before 1818) representing the women of the eighteenth century engaged in spinning, weaving, sewing, and embroidery. Lady Hong, the mother of King Chŏngjo (reign 1726-1800), wrote in her memoirs, *Hanjungnok,* that her mother not only wove cotton cloth for her family's consumption, but also sewed for the family as well.[3]

If spinning and weaving had been the regular tasks performed by Korean women of all classes, sewing and embroidery had been an even more important part of their daily life. The famous woman painter and poet, Lady Sin Saimdang (1504-1551), homesick for her parents, wrote a poem in which she expressed how much she yearned 'to sit beside my mother and sew with her.'[4] Women of the Chosŏn dynasty were said to have seven close companions: a ruler, a pair of scissors, a needle, thread, a thimble, a small iron with a long wooden handle (*indu,* a narrow, elongated triangle kept in the ashes in the brazier), and finally a regular iron (*tarimi*, a flat-bottomed bowl which held hot charcoal). This tarimi was used to press large pieces of cloth or entire garments.[5] How important these companions were to Chosŏn dynasty women can be seen in an essay, 'Lament for a needle', by an anonymous woman writer who had a needle which she cherished and believed would be with her for life. Unfortunately one day it broke. Thoroughly devastated, she writes:

> How regrettable, my needle, how pitiful! You were a special gift of fine quality, a thing out of the ordinary, prominent among ironware. Deft and swift like some knight-errant, straight and true like a loyal subject, your sharp point seemed to talk, your round eye seemed to see. When I embroidered phoenixes and peacocks on thick silk or thin, your wondrously agile movements seemed the workings of a spirit. No human effort could have matched you.[6]

Costume

Chinese accounts state that the ancient Koreans who lived in the areas of Manchuria and the northern part of Korea wore gowns with large sleeves and trousers. Although they preferred wearing white clothes for everyday, they wore silken brocades and embroidered fabrics on special occasions such as public gatherings or trips abroad.[7] Men and women attired in gowns with ample sleeves and trousers are, indeed, represented in large numbers in the murals of the Koguryŏ tombs of the Three Kingdoms period dating from the fourth to the seventh centuries. In the dancing scene, for instance, on the cast wall of the burial chamber of the *Tomb of the dancers,* the men are wearing waist-length, V-necked tunics or upper garments with ample sleeves, although the hunters in the famous mural of the hunting scene on the westem wall of the same tomb are shown wearing upper garments with well-fitting sleeves convenient for riding horses and performing other outdoor activitics. Both sexes wear trousers which are tied at the ankle. The women, however, wear ankle-or floor-length pleated skirts over the trousers. Unlike the uniform length of men's upper garments, the length of women's upper garments varies. For instance, the V-necked upper garments of the female dancers in the *Tomb of the dancers* come down below their knees, while those worn by the women on the east wall of the *Tomb of the twin pillars* descend slightly below their waists, and they are decorated with embroidered facing along the hem, neck, and the sleeve ends.

In 647, during the first year of Queen Chindŏk's reign (647-654), Kim Ch'unch'u who succeeded her as King Muyŏl (reign 654-661) brought back official costumes for men from China, and men of the Silla court adopted the Tang style. In 665, Tang dynasty women's clothing was introduced to Korea[8] and during the second half of the seventh century Korean women's costumes appear to have been modified following the Tang style. Although Chinese costumes ofthe Yuan and Ming dynasties had an impact on the official and royal costumes of Korea, the dress of ordinary Koreans remained more constant, becoming the basis for the traditional Korean costumes which are called the *hanbok -the ch'ima* and *chŏgori* (skirt and blouse or jacket) combination for women and the *paji* and *chŏgori* (tousers and jacket) combination for men.

Ch'ima and *Chŏgori*

The basic Korean costume (*hanbok*) for women consists of skirts (*ch'ima*) and blouses or jackets (*chŏgori*). Women's skirts have changed little in style since the Three Kingdoms period. They are always gathered at the top. The Chosŏn dynasty women of the gentry (*yangban*) class wore long, full skirts made of luxurious fabrics with self-patterned designs, woven or pressed gold decorations, or embroidered designs. Genre paintings of courtesans of the late Chosŏn dynasty, who dressed like the women of the gentry class, show the voluminous silhouette of their fashionable skirts. Unlike the upper class women or the courtesans, women of the lower class wore their skirts short (calf length), undoubtedly for practical purposes, since they had to perform strenuous daily tasks. The women's blouses of the Chosŏn dynasty evolved from the Three Kingdoms period. Unlike men's upper garments, women's blouses became short beginning in the seventeenth century, and during the late eighteenth and the nineteenth centuries, despite the sharp criticism voiced by men,[9] women preferred very short blouses barely covering their breasts as can be seen in the genre paintings by Kim Hongdo (1745-before 1818) and Sin Yunbok (late eighteenth century)

Paji and *Chŏgori*

Just as the basic hanbok of Korean women are skirts (*chi'ma*) and the blouses or jackets (*chŏgori*), those of Korean men are trousers (*paji*) and jackets (*chŏgori*). The loose-fitting trousers are tied at the ankle as they had been during the Three Kingdoms period as shown in the Koguryŏ murals. Over the centuries the length of men's jackets became slightly shorter coming down only to the waist by the Chosŏn dynasty. When the men of the gentry (*yangban*) class stepped out of their house, they alway put on a coat (*turumagi*) over their *paji* and *chŏgori*. Men's clothes were always designed and sewn by the women of each family or seamstresses in their employ until the introduction of Western clothes in the late nineteenth century.

Wŏnsam

The name *wŏnsam* is derived from the round neckline of the robe (*wŏn* means 'round'; sam means 'robe'). During the beginning of the Chosŏn dynasty, this robe was worn by the queen every day; by princesses and wives of court officials on ceremonial occasions; and by ordinary women on their wedding day. It has voluminous sleeves and its front comes down only to the knee, while its back covers the ankles. The colour of the garment was strictly regulated. Originally red was reserved for the queen, but in the late Chosŏn dynasty, yellow came to be the colour for the queen, while red was for the crown princess, purple for the king's secondary consorts, and green for the princesses and the wives of court officials. The queen's yellow ceremonial robe was lined in red silk with blue borders, and its sleeves had two narrow bands of red and blue attached to the main part of the yellow section. The sleeve ends were in white. The silk usually had self-patterned designs of floral and Chinese character motifs in gold threads. The queen also wore a red belt made of silk with self-patterned cloud and phoenix designs in gold thread as well as four ernbroidered dragon medallions, one sewn on the chest, one on the back, and one on each shoulder.

The earliest extant *wŏnsam* is made of green silk with woven gold decoration which belonged to Lady Chŏnggyŏng, wife of Yi Tanha (1649-1689). Another *wŏnsam* belonging to Princess Tŏkon (1822-1844) the third daughter of King Sunjo (reign 1800-1834) is also made of green silk, but decorated with pressed, rather than woven gold designs. Other extant *wŏnsam* robes are mostly in green silk without gold embellishment.[10] When the *wŏnsam* robe was used as a wedding dress by both the gentry (*yangban*) and ordinary (*sangmin*) classes during the Chosŏn dynasty, it had multi-coloured sleeves made of bands in the order of red, blue, yellow, green, red, and white. A long red belt decorated with pressed gold desings was worn below the breast line. The *wŏnsam* is still worn by the bride at a traditional Korean wedding ceremony and at the time when she presents herself formally to her parents-in-law in a ceremony called *p'aebaek*.

Hwarrot

Meaning 'flower robe', the *hwarrot* was also used as a wedding robe by the court and the gentry class during the early part of the Chosŏn dynasty. Toward the end of the dynasty, however, it was worn by brides of all classes. Made of red sillk with blue lining, its colours symbolise the *yin* and *yang*, male and female, positive and negative, and light and dark, symbolic of a harmonious world in the East Asian cosmology. It is luxuriously embroidered with auspicious floral motifs together with auspicious bird and insect designs. The most prominent floral motif is the lotus which was originally associated with Buddhism but came to symbolise in the minds of ordinary Koreans not only purity and rebirth, but also longevity and good fortune. The peony, representing wealth and honor, is another common flower, as are plum flowers and the Rose of Sharon. The most auspicious bird is the phoenix, believed to appear only during the time of peace and prosperity. If, therefore, there was no sign of the phoenix, the ruler lacked the necessary virtues to govern the people and land and no longer had the mandate of heaven. Even today Korea's presidential seal is composed of two phoenixes symbolising the wise leadership under which the nation and its people prosper in peace. The phoenix also symbolises the feminine aspect and the empress in East Asian cosmology. When used on a bridal robe it bestows the bride, the most honoured woman of the day, with fortune and prestige. Other commonly embroidered animal motifs include ducks, which symbolise conjugal fidelity and felicity, and butterflies, the much loved insects in Korea which represent vitality, love and happiness.

Together with these auspicious floral, bird and insect motifs, two sets of Chinese character phrases are embroidered on the front and the back of the robe. On the front are three-character phrases, *suyŏsan* and *puyŏhae*, meaning 'long life (as tall or long) as mountains' and 'wealth (as wide and abundant) as oceans'. On the back are four-character phrases, *Yisŏng chihap* and *paekbok chiwŏn*, together meaning 'the union of two families (is) the root of myriad happiness'. It seems appropriate that the robe, so abundantly decorated with good wishes, should be worn by a bride on her wedding day, the threshold of her new life. In its stlye the *hwarrot* resembles the *wŏnsam*. Cut like the *wŏnsam*, the *hwarrot* comes only to knee in front while the back covers the ankles. The five-colour sleeves are connected at the shoulder with a large section in red, the same as the colour of the bodice, followed by bands in blue, yellow and pink, and a white sleeve-end embroidered with flowers and birds

Tang'ui

The name *tang'ui* refers to the style of the Chinese Tang dynasty costume, but the actual garment resembles more closely the long blouses worn by women of the Koguryŏ Kingdom as represented in their tomb murals. Although generally considered to be a princesses blouse, the *tang'ui* was worn by court ladies every day and by the women of the gentry class on special occasions. Because the bodice is long and narrow, the front and back are not sewn together, but separated. As a rule, in cold weather heavy silk fabrics (*tan*) such as *mobun-tan* were used, while in warm weather lighter silk fabrics (*sa*) such as *kapsa* were chosen. Green or greenish-blue was the preferred colour for *tang'ui*.

Chobok

Although the *chobok* began as the court officials' attire for the morning audience with the king, hence the name *cho* (morning) and *bok* (attire), it became the attire for court officials on aupicious ceremonial occasions. From 1412 during the early Chosŏn dynasty, court officials from the fist to the ninth grades were allowed to wear *chobok*, but from the middle of the Chosŏn dynasty only those from the first to the fourth grades were permitted to wear *chobok*, which consisted of *chŏkch'oui* (red coat), *chŏngch'oui* (blue coat), *hunsang* (apron) and *husu* (insignia).

Wrapping cloths

Korean wrapping cloths (*pojagi*) of unusual beauty occupied a prominent place in the daily lives of Koreans of all classes during the Chosŏn dynasty (1392-1910). Although *pojagi* had been in use for centuries, all the surviving examples date from the Chosŏn dynasty except for the one *pojagi* covering the table used by the illustrious Buddhist priest, Taegak Kuksa, Uich'ŏn (1055-1101).[11] The earliest extant Chosŏn dynasty *pojagi* are the seven wrapping cloths made in 1415 by Lady Yi to wrap and cover Buddhist sutras her husband, Yu Kŭn, had copied. Three out of these seven are embroidered wrapping cloths decorated with designs of lotuses and other flowers, Tang scrolls, grasses, reeds, clouds and cranes. They are now in the collection of Chŏnju Provincial Museum.[12] Another early wrapping cloth which has survived was used in 1681 on the occasion of the wedding of princess Myŏng'an (1665-1687), King Hyŏnjong's (reign 1659-1674) daughter, to O T'aeje.[13]

Pojagi were used for wrapping as well as for covering, storing, and carrying objects. They were used for objects small and large, ordinary and precious. *Pojagi* served a variety of purposes, from covering a food table, to draping a Confucian or Buddhist altar, to wrapping a sacred text. Lady Hong wrote in the aforementioned memoirs that when she returned home from the palace after having been selected as the wife of the Crown Prince Sado, not only was she brought 'through the gate reserved for male visitors' and received by her parents attired in ceremonial robes, but she also noticed that 'the table was covered with a scarlet cover'[14] as was done on special occasions. Covering a table or an altar signified the importance of the occasion as wrapping an object represented not only an individual's concern for that which was being wrapped, but also respect for its receiver. There was an unspoken folk belief that by wrapping an object, *pok* (good fortune) could be enclosed or captured within a *pojagi*.[15] Special events such weddings, therefore, required a whole set of new *pojagi*.

Pojagi are generally square in shape. On rare occasions, however, they are made in rectangular shapes. Depending upon their use, *pojagi* came in varying sizes ranging from one *p'ok* (about 35cm) to ten *p'ok*. The *pojagi* used for wrapping a goose which the groom's family presented to the bride's before the wedding ceremony, were small, measuring approximately one *p'ok* square. In contrast the *pojagi* used for wrapping bedding were usually ten times larger.

Silk, gossamer, cotton, and ramie were popularly used to make wrapping cloths, in colours ranging from red, purple, blue, green, yellow and pink, to dark blue and white. The construction and embellishment of *pojagi* were also diverse. Some were lined, others unlined; some were padded or quilted. Some were decorated with embroidery, painting, patchwork or paper-thin gold sheets.

The most outstanding examples, from an aesthetic perspective, are the embroidered and patchwork wrapping cloths. The embroidered motifs are based on trees, flowers, birds, clouds, fruits, dragons, phoenixes and ideographs. They are freely represented, making the embroidered designs often burst forth with a sense of abandon. When small pieces of cloth in different colours were used to make patchwork *pojagi*, the beauty evident in the intricacy of the patchwork and skillful balancing and contrasting of colours are reminiscent of the abstract compositions of Piet Mondrian (1872-1944) and Paul Klee (1879-1940). Long before these Western painters were renouncing the art of illusionism and discovering true reality in rectilinear purism based on a severely limited vocabulary of forms and colours, Korean women had discovered the beauty in abstract two-dimensional designs.They must have experienced the joys of making beautiful designs as well as the spiritual rewards of creative activities. The works which best show the makers' unusually refined aesthetic sensibility are those made with transparent pieces of ramie.They created two-dimensional abstract designs of breathtaking beauty by fitting together different sizes of asymmetrical shapes. The effect of these pieces is completely modern. Without exception, *pojagi* were made by women. In a rigidly Confucian era, when women were taught to follow the 'Three Tenets of Obedience' and discouraged from engaging in any form of intellectual pursuit, women artists unknown to us today poured their creative energies into making these stunning works which reflect their own individual sense of harmony and beauty.The *pojagi* and their anonymous makers form a fascinating counterpart to the unknown Korean potters of the Chosŏn dynasty, all men, whose ceramics are now famous throughout the world.

Wrapping cloths can be divided first into two large groups according to their users-*kung po* (wrapping cloths for the palace) and *min po* (wrapping cloths for the people). They can be divided further according to their construction, design and the purpose they serve. If they are lined, they are called *kyŏp po* (*kyŏp* means 'double'), while unlined ones are called *hot po* (*hot* means 'single'). Those made to wrap fragile objects are often padded with cotton and therefore called *som po* (*som* means 'cotton'), while quilted wrapping cloths are called *nubi po* (*nubi* means 'to quilt'). If they are made with a patchwork design, they are called *chogak po* (*chogak* means 'small segments'), while embroidered wrapping cloths are called *su po* (*su* means 'embroidery'). If they are made to wrap bedding, they are called *yibul po* (*yibul* means 'bedding'). Those for wrapping fabrics are *ch'ŏn po* (*ch'ŏn* means 'fabrics') and those for enclosing clothing are called *oppo* (*ot* means 'clothes'. When it is followed by the word *po*, it changes to *op* in sound becoming *oppo*). Thus, depending on the purposes they serve, they can be named accordingly. A *pojagi*, therefore, can have more than one name. For instance, if it is a lined piece in a patchwork design made to cover a food table, it can be called by three different names-*kyŏp po* (lined wrapping cloth), *chogak po* (patchwork wrapping cloth) and *sang po* (food table wrapping cloth). The names of better known wrapping cloths and their characteristics follow.

Kung po

Pojagi had been made for the palace-not only to wrap objects for protection and safe-keeping, but also to show the proper respect due to those who were to be the recipients of the wrapped articles. Each year a variety of wrapping cloths was produced in large numbers for palace use by the bureau (*Sang'uiwŏn*) assigned to oversee all sewing needs at the palace.[16] *Sangbang chŏngnye*, a three-volume work written in 1752, lists in detail all the items which had to be presented each year to the king and queen, and the crown prince and princess on their birthdays, on New Year's Day, on the fifteenth day of the eighth lunar month, and on other special days.

This book not only enumerates the clothing, headgear and footwear required for different occasions, but also stipulates the colours, fabrics, thread and other materials for their manufacture. And a wrapping cloth had to be made for each item ranging in its size from one *p'ok* to eight *p'ok*. Of 235 wrapping cloths listed in *Sangbang chŏngnye*, the smallest wrapping cloths were used to enclose headbands, silver spoons, and personal ornaments, and the largest ones for wrapping folding screens and chests. The types of the wrapping cloths made for palace use were *hop po* (unlined wrapping cloths), *kyŏp po* (lined wrapping cloths), *som po* (wrapping cloths padded with cotton), *nubi po* (wrapping cloths quilted with parallel lines), *sikji po* (wrapping cloths made entirely with oiled paper), and *tangch'ae po* (wrapping cloths with painted decorations). The colours for the palace wrapping cloths were in order of preference: red, purple, blue, green and white.[17]

The Kungjungpalgi (Palace Record) gives a record of *kung po* used in 1882 at the wedding of King Sunjong (reign 1907-1910). It shows that both lined and unlined wrapping cloths were made to enclose the various wedding gifts, and *nubi po* to cover food and food tables. Although more ramie and cotton fabrics, rather than silk, were used, their colours were more varied compared to the colours listed in *Sangbang chŏngnye* in which a definite preference for the red hues could be detected.[18]

The earliest extant *kung po* of the Chosŏn dynasty, as it has been mentioned, is the one used in 1681 on the occasion of the wedding of Princess Myŏng'an daughter of King Hyŏnjong (1659-1674), to O T'aeje. It is a *kyŏp po* of blue silk patterned with the cloud and seven-treasures design. Three *p'ok* square, it is lined with plain blue silk. The Ch'angdŏk Palace Collection now holds about one hundred *kung po* all of them made during the late Chosŏn dynasty.[19]

Min Po

Pojagi had also been an indispensable part of the daily life of the common people before the introduction of such things as suitcases, carrying bags and screens for windows and doors. Many different types of wrapping cloths used every day by ordinary people are called *min po,* meaning people's wrapping cloths as opposed to those made for and used by royalty. A *min po* often served more than a single purpose, and therefore the same *min po* would be called by different names. The most numerous *min po* were the *chogak po* (patchwork wrapping cloths), *su po* (embroidered wrapping cloths), and *sang po* (wrapping cloths made to cover food tables).

Chogak po

The most popular wrapping cloths used exclusively by the common people were the *chogak po*-wrapping cloths with patchwork designs, which were made with small pieces of leftover cloth. The patchwork wrapping cloths perhaps reveal most accurately the world of Korean women of the Chosŏn dynasty. Korean women, taught from an early age to be patient and frugal, saved even the smallest pieces of silk, cotton or ramie cloth when they designed, cut and sewed their family members' clothes. And when they found some quiet time, they brought out these colourful remnants and spread them out on the floor. They would separate these small pieces into different groups according to their weight-heavy silk pieces, light gauze-like silk pieces, ramie pieces, and so on. They would also ponder over the fabrics with and without self-patterned designs. They would then cut them into appropriate shapes such as squares, rectangles, triangles and trapezoids, and match these forms and their colours until everything looked just right to them. While the initial process of laying out forms and colours provided an opportunity for Chosŏn dynasty women to test their own aesthetic sensibilities and discover their innate creative talents, the actual sewing must have been akin to sutra copying or painting multi-images of Buddhas or Bodhisattvas. As the copiers of Buddhist sutras and the painters of Buddhist images believed that each character and each image of the Buddha brought them additional merit and placed the Pure Land of the Buddha Amitabha ever closer to their reach, the makers of the patchwork wrapping cloths must similarly have believed that blessings and happiness (*pok*) accumulated with each stitch and each piece they added. Unlike the sutra copiers or painters of the Buddha images, however, whose activities were meant to benefit themselves and their sponsors, the good wishes of the makers of patchwork wrapping cloths were aimed at the receivers of their works. The sincere prayers and wishes of the mothers, grandmothers, and aunts who pieced together the patchwork wrapping cloths were directed to the happiness of their sons and daughters, nieces and nephews, and grandchildren. Many patchwork wrapping cloths have never been used, perhaps indicating that their recipients knew them to be the tangible signs of affection and good wishes of the makers and wanted to keep and remember their love and blessings forever. Since no *kung po* made with a patchwork design has survived or been recorded, we can assume that wrapping cloths made from small remnants had no place in the palace, and that they were the exclusive creation of and for the ordinary people.

Su po

Together with patchwork wrapping cloths, embroidered wrapping cloths were also popular judging from the extant examples. They were used only for happy occasions such as betrothals and marriages. *Su po* made in the Kangnŭng area in the central east are especially spectacular because of the jubilant natural forms embroidered in brilliant colours. The most frequently used motifs were trees and flowers followed by fruits, butterflies and birds. In Korea trees have had sacred symbolism from the earliest times. In the foundation myth of Korea, the celestial prince Hwan'ung comes down with his followers to Mt T'aebaek 'to a spot under a tree by the Holy Altar'.[20] The famous gold crowns of the Silla Kingdom (57 BC -AD 668) are decorated with one or more stylised trees which symbolise the tree of life. Ancient Koreans also believed that the sacred tree connected heaven and earth. Flowers symbolised wealth, prosperity and honor while fruits symbolised abundance in material things and male offspring. Birds and butterflies were frequently used to represent happiness and joy.

The fabric on which embroidery was done was often cotton, while lining fabrics were silk. Today the designs are frequently copied directly on to the fabrics. During the Chosŏn dynasty, however,they were first drawn or printed on a thick Korean paper. This was then placed over the fabric and the embroidery was done over the paper which provided extra padding under the embroidered designs. The parts of the paper not covered by the embroidery fell off easily due to needle marks made around each design. Blue, green, red, pink, orange, yellow, black and white were the dominant palette making the design burst forth with a feeling of exuberance and abandon.

Although the design motifs are based on natural forms, they are flattened and simplified, so that they can easily be viewed as abstract designs. A tree spreads out its branches vigorously in all directions laden with broad leaves as if to empower the whole world with energy and joy. In this imaginary land of hope and happiness, tree leaves come in rainbow colours, and small birds perched on the branches are also yellow, orange, red, pink and blue-representing the embroiderer's wishes for the recipient's happiness and prosperity in her new married life. Embroidered wrapping cloths, more than any other type, encouraged the full use of the makers' imaginative talent. This can be seen in their composition and forms as well as in their use of colour. The tree branches, for instance, grow as if they are not bound by earthly logic and the leaves metamorphose into birds. The colours of trees, leaves, birds, flowers, and other forms in the compositions are not only completely arbitrary but full of excitement and vitality because they represent the land of the makers' imagination which is free from the established rules of the world.

Sang po

The wrapping cloths made to cover the food table are called *sang po*. During pre-modern times they not only kept food warm, but also protected it from flies and other insects. *Sang po* were most frequently made with patchwork designs and always had a small knob in the centre for easylifting, although not all the wrapping clothes with a central knob were made exclusively to cover food tables. Some *sang po* had long sashes attached to the four corners so that they could be tied under the portable food tables or trays on windy or rainy days. Because strict Confucian rules of propriety had to be observed between the sexes during the Chosŏn dynasty, the men's quarters called the *sarang-ch'ae* (outer quarters) were separated from the women's quarters, the *an-ch'ae* (inner quarters), where the kitchen was located. Light material such as ramie (*moshi*) was often used for summer and thick fabrics which sometimes were padded with cotton were favoured for winter. Those *sang po* in constant use were usually lined with an additional oiled paper to protect them from being soiled by food.

Sikji po

All *pojagi* are made of cloth with one exception. One type of *sang po* is made exclusively of oiled paper, and hence the name *sikji po*. Serving as the covers or wrappers of food or food tables, they come in square and rectangular shapes. Square *sikji po* in the size of one *p'ok* usually have a long sash at the centre and appear to have been used to wrap a small portion of food for outings or travels. Those in a rectagular shape have their four corners folded to fit over rectangular tables or trays. Both square and rectangular covers and wrappers are decorated symmetrically with floral, bat, butterfly and geometric designs made from cut-out oiled paper in red and black, making a pleasant contrast to the light yellow main portion of *sikji po*, which is similar to the oiled paper used for the *ondol* floor of Korean homes. The central knob of *sikji po* attached for easy lifting is made of braided paper.

Kirŏgi po

Meaning the 'wrapping cloth for a goose', *kirŏgi po* are used to wrap a wooden goose which was presented by the bridegroom's family to the bride's family to be placed on the central table during the traditional Korean wedding ceremony. For *kirŏgi po* red and blue colours were used which symbolised *yin* and *yang. The kirŏgi po* were not only lined and embroidered, but also decorated often with multi-strands of rainbow-coloured threads representing rice stalks, a symbol of the family's wishes for abundance in married life.

Yemul po

As a part of the betrothal ritual on a specially picked day which is most auspicious for the new couple, the bridegroom's family sends the bride's family a letter and a gift of fabrics usually of silk for the bride as a formal acknowledgment of the forthcoming marriage. They are enclosed in a special wrapping cloth called *yemul po* (*yemul* means 'ceremonial or special object').

Yedan po

The wrapping cloths made to enclose the gifts the bride'sfamily sent to the groom's family are called *yedan po*. Made in red and blue silk, *yedan po* measure approximately two or three *p'ok* depending on the financial resources of the bride's family.

Norigae po

Measuring about one *p'ok* square and made of silk, the *norigae po* are made to protect personal ornaments, *norigae*, and hence the name *norigae po*. In order to protect the precious and often fragile items, these are usually padded with cotton. Two sashes are attached at one corner to tie them securely. They are often decorated with embroidery.

Kŭmbak po

Wrapping cloths decorated with designs in pressed gold are called *kŭmbak po* (*kŭmbak* means 'pressed gold'). Although such opulent decorations had been ordinarily limited to the use of royalty, commoners who could afford the expense were permitted to use them only on the special occasion of a wedding. Not only floral designs, but also designs of dragons and phoenixes were used to make them as luxurious and prestigious as those used by royalty.

Conclusion

Although Koreans are often referred to as the 'people of white clothes' (*paekui minjok*), they made vibrant colours an important part of their lives reflecting their energy and vitality in the celebration of life, and their ardent wish for joy ănd happiness. It is fascinating that Korean costumes retain many features which can be traced back to the Three Kingdoms period (BC 57-668 AD). Korean men's traditional clothing, *paji and chŏgori*, especially has the appearance of a riding costume, showing the close connection between the Koreans and the ancient horse-riding people of North Asia and the Steppes. The Korean women's costume, *ch'ima and chŏgori*, has been praised for the elegance of the skirt's flowing lines and the simplicity of the short blouse accented with long sashes, often in contrasting colours. Even today women are the tenacious keepers of tradition, making sure to wear the traditional *hanbok* on special occasions such as weddings, birthday celebrations, New Year's Day, and the *ch' usŏk* (the full moon day of the eighth lunar month).

The creative talents of Korean women during the Chosŏn dynasty can perhaps be best illustrated by the wrapping cloths they made. It is clear that these unknown women, who lived in an extremely rigid society, delighted in their creative activity, often discovering their hidden talents while working on their projects. Their strong emotions as well as their good wishes for the recipients of these wrapping cloths show through the exuberant colours and designs of their patchwork and embroidery. Their unusually refined aesthetic sensibility is best captured in the arrangement of lines and shapes of ramie pieces. These wrapping cloths in monochrome and in a 'profusion of colour' are the legacies of the creative unknown Chosŏn dynasty women to the world.

Kumja Paik Kim is Curator of Korean Art, Asian Art Museum of San Francisco, USA.

Notes

1. Peter H Lee, *Sourcebook of Korean Civilization*, vol 1, Columbia University Press, New York, 1993, p 57; Kim Pusik, *Samguk sagi* (History of the Three Kingdoms Period), Yi Pyŏng-do, ed, 2 vols, Uryu Munhwasa, Seoul, 1977, 1:5.
2. Han Yonhwa, *Chŏnt'ong Chasu* (Traditional Embroidery), Taewŏn-sa, Seoul, 1989, p 74; Kim Yongsuk, *Han'guk yŏsoksa* (History of the Customs and Manners of Korean Women), Minŭmsa, Seoul, 1989, p 42.
3. Yang-hi Choe-Wall, tr, *Memoirs of a Korean Queen, Lady Hong,* KPI, London & New York, 1985, p 3.
4. Kichung Kim, 'Chosŏn dynasty women seen through their own eyes', *Profusion of colour: Korean costumes and wrapping cloths of the Chosŏn dynasty*, exhibition catalogue, Asian Art Museum of San Francisco, 1995, p 18.
5. Peter H Lee, *Anthology of Korean Literature*, The University Press of Hawaii, Honolulu, 1981, p 249.
6. *Ibid*, p 248.
7. Peter H Lee, *Sourcebook*, pp 7-24.
8. Kim Yongsuk, p 43.
9. Suk Joo-Sun (Sŏk Chusŏn), 'Han'guk Poksik ui Pyŏnch'ŏn, (Evolution of Korean costumes), *Han'guk ui Mi* (Beauty of Korea: traditional costumes, ornaments and cloth wrappings), exhibition catalogue, National Museum of Korea, Seoul, 1988, p 124.
10. *Ibid,* p 128.
11. Han Yŏnghwa, *op cit*, p 78. Taegak Kuksa, Uich'ŏn, was the fourth son of King Munjong of the Koryŏ dynasty. This wrapping cloth is decorated with a dragon design and is in the Sŏn'am-sa monastery in Sŭngju, South Chŏlla province.
12. Han Sangsu, 'Hanguk Chasu Yŏn'gu Ilhwan' (Survey on the studies of Korean embroidery), *Hanjung Kogŭm Chasu Kyoryu-jŏn* (Art of embroidery: relationship between Korea and China throughout succesive periods), exhibition catalogue, Traditional Craftwork Museum, Kyŏngbok Palace, Seoul, 9-25 March 1991, p 96.
13. Huh Dong-hwa, 'Yet Pojagi' (Traditional wrapping cloths), *Han'guk ui Mi*, exhibition catalogue, National Museum of Korea, Seoul, 1988, p 145; Huh Dong-hwa, *The wonder cloth*, The Museum of Korean Embroidery, Seoul, 1988, p 267.
14. Yang-hi Choe-Wall, tr, *Memoirs*, p 7.
15. Huh Dong-hwa, *The wonder cloth*, p 274; Yi, Song-Mi, *Korean costumes and textiles*, exhibition catalogue, IBM Gallery of Science and Art, New York, 14 April-13 June 1992, p 16.
16. Huh Dong-hwa, *The wonder cloth*, pp 266-272.
17. *Ibid*, pp 267-269.
18. *Ibid.*
19. *Ibid*, p 270.
20. Peter H Lee, *Sourcebook,* p 6.
21. Huh Dong-hwa, *The wonder cloth*, pp 270-271.

History and art in traditional wrapping cloths

Huh Dong-hwa

The Korean people have long used square cloths or *pojagi* to wrap, carry and cover things. The cloths are practical in that they are much easier and cheaper to make than wooden boxes or chests, and they have the added advantage of taking up very little space when they are not in use. In addition to their practical value, *pojagi* have also been used by all classes of traditional Korean society as an expression of respect for others as well as for the items which are wrapped. The care taken in wrapping even the most humble item reflects the giver's appreciation for the recipient and for the item itself. The prevalence of *pojagi* as a sign of respect even today is clearly illustrated by such simple acts as the wrapping of the *ham*, the box of gifts given by the groom's family to the family of the bride on the eve of a wedding, and its contents and the delivery of important government documents to the National Assembly wrapped in brightly coloured *pojagi.*

Traditional folk belief has also played a role in the popularity of the *pojagi as* Koreans have long believed that *pok* (good luck or happiness) can be preserved inside the wrapping cloths, thus making them important components in many traditional ceremonies and rituals.

Traditional *pojagi* are classified according to their use, the status of their user, their design and their composition. Perhaps the two most basic categories are the *kung po*, which refers to the *pojagi* used in the royal court, and the *min po*, which refers to the *pojagi* used by ordinary people.

An examination of *kung po* reveals a clear picture of life in the royal court of the Chosŏn dynasty (1392-1910). According to court records, most *kung po* were made from domestic cloth, pink and red silk being the most favoured fabrics. The Chosŏn royals' preference for these colours was in part a reflection of their desire to avoid the use of yellow which symbolised Chinese royalty. Red was favoured because it was similar to purple, the state colour of the Chosŏn dynasty which was restricted for use by the royal family alone.

The different sizes of *kung po* are also described, each having its own specific use. *Pojagi* are measured in *p'ok*, about a 35 cm unit, and thus were classified as for example one *p'ok kung po* or two *p'ok kung po.* A one *p'ok kung po* may be used to store silverware or small utensils used in wedding ceremonies, while an eight *p'ok kung po*, the largest used by the royal family or aristocrats at court, might be used to wrap as many as four cotton quilts or two mattresses for the wedding of the crown prince.

The commoners' *min po* were much simpler than *kung po,* tended to be more abstract in decoration and were stronger, as they needed to be used over and over again. While many *min po* were multipurpose, others were reserved for use on special occasions. Like *kung po, min po* reveal a great deal about the lives of their creators.

Several types of *min po* were used when performing Buddhist rites in temples or at the homes of believers. The *kongyang po* was a piece of white cloth spread over the table bearing the regular meal offered to the Buddha, while the *maji po* or *sasi po* were used to cover the food offered at a particular time in the morning. A *kyŏng-jon po* was used to wrap and protect the Buddhist scriptures. The care taken in the sewing and use of these *pojagi* reflects their creators reverence for the Buddha himself.

Other cloths were designated for use in marriage rites. The *kirŏgi po* was used to wrap the wooden goose which was handed to the bride as a token of everlasting love during the marriage ceremony, while the *p'yepaek po* was used to wrap and cover the food presented by the bride to the elders in the groom's family. The *pojagi* used in marriage ceremonies tended to be made of red and blue silk representing the bride and groom, *yin* and *yang,* respectively.

In addition to these ceremonial *pojagi*, there were also hundreds of *min po* used in everyday life. *Pojagi* were used as book bags for school children, suitcases by travellers, closets for clothing out of season, covers for clothing out of season, covers for small tables bearing food, stationary holders for important documents and letters. *Pojagi* were not only practical and inexpensive, they also reflected a reverence for the items which they covered. Thus schoolmasters always wrapped their rods in silk *pojagi* in order to impress upon the children that the rods were used for their improvement rather than aimless punishment; and gifts were always wrapped carefully as a sign of respect for the recipient.

Perhaps the most appealing type of *min po* is the *chogak po*, a mosaic cloth made from left-over scraps of material. While *chogak po* vary in size according to their purpose, they were generally made to cover food. *Chogak po* were pieced together from scraps of fabric left over after sewing, much like the patchwork quilts found in the West.

Over half of the *chogak po* which survive today show no trace of use. They have been handed down from mother to daughter over the generations as a kind of keepsake. What inspired Korean women to make these complicated art works? Certainly the joy of creating a piece of beauty played an important part in the development of this art form. Unlike patchwork quilts, which were often the fruit of a sociable quilting bee, traditional Korean *chogak po* were the creation of hundreds of individual women sitting alone in their rooms with little contact with the outside world.

Most of the *chogak po* which survive today date back to the second half of the 19th century and the early 20th century. They are generally made of machine-woven silk, sometimes imported, although many examples of *chogak po* made of ramie, a roughly woven cloth made from the fibres of an Asian shrub, hemp and cotton also exist. *Chogak po* made of loosely woven silk, thin silk, ramie or hemp were used in the summer months to protect food from flies and dust while permitting the free circulation of air. Quilted and lined *pojagi* were used in the winter to keep foods warm. Many *chogak po*, as well as most other table-sized *pojagi*, had long straps on each corner so that the *pojagi* could be tied down to prevent the cover from falling off when the table was carried. A tag-like handle made of cloth was usually affixed to the centre of the *pojagi* for easy removal.

While the texture created by the different fabrics contributed to the beauty of each *chogak po*, perhaps the single most striking feature of these patchwork pieces is their harmonious use of colour. The choice and arrangement of colours make each *chogak po* unique and reflect the personality of the creator. Many of the patterns are asymmetrical, although the recurrent use of colour provides balance within the work, while other designs are regular and precise. Some have the appearance of a checkerboard while others are made of hundreds of colourful triangles, sometimes arranged in a regular diagonal pattern and sometimes seemingly at random. Other *chogak po* have a graduated pattern in which a square of fabric in the centre is surrounded with pieces which increase in size as they radiate outward. One of the most complicated designs is the *cintamani* or 'wishing stone' *chogak po* in which circles of fabric are overlapped and folded in a regular pattern, creating a flower petal effect.

While most *chogak po* display a certain degree of regularity in pattern, many, particularly of the unlined variety, reveal no visual rhyme or reason, much like the American 'crazy quilt'. Still, the intricate linking of the irregular scraps of cloth often results in works of art which echo the beauty of the abstract paintings of Paul Klee and his early 20th century compatriots.

Many *chogak po* are decorated with small knots shaped like tiny bats. These bat decorations are made of scraps of fabric and are sewn to the seams of quilted *pojagi* to hold the two layers together and to the centre and corners of unlined *chogak po*. These decorations break the visual monotony of the *pojagi* and also are believed to bring good luck as the Chinese character for bat is phonetically similar to that for good fortune (*pok*). Also it is possible that representations of the bat were used to repel the evil spirits that bring bad fortune.

Su po or embroidered *pojagi* have been treasured as family heirlooms handed down from generation to generation. Their value lies not only in their exquisite handiwork, but also in their embodiment of folk belief. The patterns depicted in embroidered *pojagi* symbolise the pursuit of happiness and good luck and as a result were treasured from generation to generation.

Judging from their fluid patterns and the use of machine-woven cotton fabric for the backing of embroidered *pojagi*, it appears that this genre became prevalent toward the end of the Chosŏn dynasty when machine-woven cloth was easily obtained and the rigid aesthetic perfectionism of the early Chosŏn period had relaxed somewhat.

Five basic colours - blue, red, yellow, white and black - were used in embroidered *pojagi* together with some gold and intermediary colours. These basic colours reflected the traditional principle of *yin* and *yang*; the warm colours representing the sun, fire and blood, while the blue and greens suggested trees, grass, birth, growth and prosperity. These five colours also correspond to the four points of the compass and the centre; the five elements of the weather (cold, warmth, wind, dryness and humidity); the five elements of the universe (wood, fire, metal, water and earth); the five seasonal differences (spring, summer, autumn, winter and *toyong*, the 18 transitional days preceding each season); and the five blessings (longevity, wealth, success, health and luck).

The figures and designs portrayed in embroidered *pojagi* also hold deep symbolic significance. The layers of intricate stitching portray flowers, trees, birds such as cranes, phoenix and peacocks, and insects such as butterflies and grasshoppers, each expressing the desire for happiness and good fortune as well as a belief in the spiritual power of objects and creatures found in nature.

The use of oiled paper in the *kung po* mentioned above was also common in *min po* from the Chosŏn period. One type was made entirely of oiled paper; a more common variety had cloth, sometimes quilted or embroidered, on one side and oiled paper on the other. These paper *pojagi* were sometimes decorated with designs cut from coloured paper which were then applied to the corners and folds.

Pojagi were also decorated with Chinese mineral paints applied to ramie or cotton. The whole surface was covered with patterns including flowers, birds and the Chinese characters for peace, prosperity and longevity as well as symbols of eternal life and prosperity such as phoenix, peonies and chrysanthemums.

Other *min po* were adorned with woodblock prints bearing these popular motifs. The cloth to be printed was laid on a plain wooden board and the block with the pattern was placed on top. The patterns were carved so that the edges would match and the intersection between each print would not show.

Every traditional *pojagi* which survives today is treasured as a unique expression of the character of the nameless woman who created it.

Huh Dong-hwa is Director of The Museum of Korea Embroidery, Seoul, Korea

Women in Korean history and art

Yi Sŏng-mi

The magnificent and refined costumes and wrapping cloths shown in this exhibition are works created exclusively by women of the late Chosŏn dynasty (1392-1910). Typically, they are anonymous creations, yet they are among the most celebrated artistic endeavors in Korean history. Viewers of these exquisite *ch'imsŏn* (literally, needle craft) works will naturally wonder who these women were. It would not be wrong to say that in old Korea women of all classes practiced embroidery and sewing. For upper-class women, it was at once an elegant pastime and a productive endeavor as all the *ch'imsŏn* items were actually used in daily life; among the lower class, women who specialised in *ch'imsŏn* were called *ch'imsŏnbi* (*bi* means 'female servant or slave') and were hired by the court or the *yangban* families to produce the tremendous amount of goods the *yangban* required.

Talented and creative as they may have been, women of the Chosŏn dynasty did not seem to have been accorded the same degree of legal and social status given to women of ancient and medieval Korea. Although women in all countries historically were treated as secondary to men, gender inequality in Chosŏn dynasty Korea was exceptionally severe and rigid. Historical evidence indicates that laws governing the social status of women in the Three Kingdoms (first to mid-seventh century) and the Unified Silla (668-935) periods, or even those of the Koryŏ dynasty (918-1392) were much less unfavorable to women than those of the Chosŏn dynasty. The adoption of neo-Confucianism as the state creed at the beginning of the Chosŏn dynasty was largely responsible for the strict enforcement of traditional Confucian mores.

In the neo-Confucian world order, everything has its own hierarchical position in the universe where it maintains a certain harmonious relationship with other beings. This view of the universe also extends to the world of man, where the most important human relationships are defined as the three netropes or *samgang:* loyalty to the ruler, filial piety, and subordination to the husband. Of these three tenets, the last concerned women most directly, subjecting women to absolute obedience to men as dictated by the moral ethics called the 'principle of three obediences' (*samjongjiŭi*): obedience to her father, to her husband, and to her son after the death of her husband. Under these principles, it was almost unthinkable for women to do anything other than her essentail duties as wife and mother of a household. *Ch'imsŏn,* therefore, was the most suitable and natural act through which a woman could express her creative talent

The following survey of women in Korean history sheds light on the lives and social milieu of the traditional Korean women who were at once creators and users of the costumes and wrapping cloths of consummate beauty illustrated in this catalogue.[1]

Korean women before the Chosŏn dynasty

During the Three Kingdoms period and the Koryŏ dynasty, women enjoyed more freedom and better social status than they did later in the Chosŏn dynasty. The fact that there were three queens, Queen Sŏndŏk (reign 632-646), Chindŏk (reign 647-653), and Chinsŏng (reign 888-897), who served as reigning monarchs is a testimony to the relatively unprejudiced social treatment of genders in ancient Korean society. The unique laws of succession to the throne in the Silla Kingdom, governed by a strict consanguineous hereditary rank system, established these women as queens.

The Silla aristocratic class system, the 'bone rank' system (*kolp'umje*) had two noble ranks, the'hallowed-bone' rank (*sŏnggol*) and the 'true-bone' rank (*chin'gol*), along with six additional classescalled *yuktup'um.*[2] At first, only the descendants of the 'hallowed-bone' rank could occupy the throne. As a result, since King Chinp'yŏng (579-632) had no son to succeed him, he decided to bequeath the throne to his daughter (later, Queen Sŏndŏk) who had displayed extraordinary intelligence since her childhood.[3]

Queen Sŏndŏk's reign was marked by illustrious achievements, some of which can still be seen in Kyŏngju, the capital of the Silla Kingdom for one thousand years. To her reign are credited the famous astronomical observatory called Ch'ŏmsŏngdae ('starwatching terrace') and the Pagoda of Punhwangsa Temple, the mock-brick pagoda of unique artistic merit. Her artistic sensibility is well demonstrated by a story recorded in *Samguk Sagi*, the official history of the Three Kingdoms.

More remarkable in terms of gender equality is the fact that Queen Sŏndŏk was succeeded by her cousin, Queen Chindŏk. Two successive female monarchs definitely implies that there was little prejudice against women as long as they were qualified in terms of both their bloodline and ability. After the extinction of the 'hallowed-bone' rank, when the country resorted to the 'true-bone' rank for its leadership under King Taejong Muyŏl (reign 654-660), who unified the Three Kingdoms, Silla people were open to having a female monarch. Although Queen Chinsŏng, the last of the three queens, was not as illustrious as her female predecessors, her mere presence in Korean history is a noteworthy contrast to the drastically lowered social status of women in the Chosŏn period.

In a broader spectrum of Silla society, a woman's right to head the family was acknowledged. Unmarried daughters were also allowed to head the family.[4] This situation is in marked contrast with the family system of the Chosŏn dynasty in which women by custom were never allowed to establish a separate household (though this was not explicitly outlined in the National Law).[5]

Intimate personal relationships between men and women, a reflection of the generally more open social atmosphere of the Three Kingdoms, are reflected in several poems portraying love affairs which, with the passage of time, became almost legendary. Among them, the poem of the love between King Mu (reign 600-651 of Paekche and Princess Sŏnhwa of Koguryŏ is well known.[6] Even more famous is the *Ch'oyŏngga*, which gently portrays in a few lines the sad illicit affair of a wife and the frustration of her husband.[7] This story was later immortalised by the powerfully expressive mask dance, *Ch'oyŏng-mu*, which is still widely performed.

Embroidery served as a pastime as well as an act of religious devotion in the Three Kingdoms period. Although all the items in this exhibition are from the Chosŏn period, literary evidence testifies to the uses of embroidery in the earlier Three Kingdoms period. *Samguk Sagi* (History of the Three Kingdoms) records a Paekche Kingdom morning ceremony during the reign of King Koi (?-286) performed at the royal court on an auspicious day in May in which wide-sleeved costumes embroidered with flowers and birds in golden threads were worn. It also records that as early as the fifth century, not only royalty but also the common people used embroidered and colourful silk.[8] Although no examples of Paekche embroidery have survived, the Tenjukoku Mandara of the Asuka period in Japan, now kept in the Chugu-ji Nunnery in Nara, can be considered a reflection of the technique of Paekche embroidery as the artistic influence of Paekche on Asuka Japan is a well-established historical fact.

The oldest existing piece of embroidery in Korea is the needle case used by Queen Sondok found inside the Punhwangsa Pagoda in Kyŏngju mentioned earlier. Queen Chindŏk is also said to have embroidered the text of the 'Ode to Peace' *(T'aepyŏng-song)* she had composed. She presented it to the Tang Emperor as a diplomatic gesture in order to seek China's aid in unifying the Koguryŏ and Paekche Kingdoms with Silla.[9] A Buddhist nun of the Unified Silla period by the name of Wŏnhae ('circular ocean') is supposed to have been the best painter and embroiderer of the country. After the death of King Hŏn'gang (reign 875-885), she is recorded to have painted and embroidered the king's portrait upon the request of his bereaved wife. She also embroidered a Buddhist banner with an image of Shakyamuni upon the request of the wife of King Chŏnggang (reign 886-887).[10]

During the Koryŏ dynasty, no woman occupied the throne as the ruling queen. However, women seemed to have enjoyed considerable freedom. Visits to Buddhist temples by all classes of women were quite common. Koryŏ women also seemed to have had significant inheritance rights. Property was divided equally among sons and daughters of a family; though this equal division of wealth among sons and daughters was not written in any law, it was a general practice after the reign of King Kojong (reign

1214-1259).[11] According to Professor Deuchler, the household wealth including the patrimonial land was divided according to the will of the father. A Koryŏ woman did not receive her share in the form of a dowry but could expect to inherit a portion of family wealth after the death of her father. Deuchler contends that this practice fostered the strong bond among siblings and granted women a high degree of economic security in Koryŏ society.[12]

Women's contributions to society in the Koryŏ dynasty were recognised as well; for example, a woman was awarded 300 *sŏk* of rice if she produced more than three sons who passed the state examinations.[13] In contrast to the extreme chastity code of the Chosŏn dynasty, whereby a widowed young woman must remain single for the rest of her life, Koryŏ women, when widowed without male offspring to support her, were expected to remarry even in upper-class society. The famous scholar of the late Koryŏ period, Yi Saek (1328-1396), wrote in the epitaph for his teacher, An Po, that it would be difficult for his widow not to remarry as she had no son to support her, reflecting that a lack of prejudice against a widow's remarriage existed.[14]

There were some negative sides to the relatively liberal situation during the Koryŏ period. For example, women flocked to temples in enormous numbers when a famous priest performed a special Buddhist sermon. During the reign of King Kongmin (reign 1351-1374), a certain priest called Naong held a Manjusuri Sermon (*munsu-hoe*) at the Hoeamsa Temple in Yangju. The temple gate was so mobbed by women enraptured with almost frantic religious fervour that the law enforcement authority had to be called in to control the scene.[15]

Some women of the scholar-official families seem to have played active roles in promoting their husbands by visiting the residences of powerful high officials during the late Koryŏ period. Their unashamed attitude resulted in censure at the early Chosŏn court. Soon after the establishment of the Chosŏn dynasty in 1392, the inspector general (*taesahŏn*) Nam Chae made a strong recommendation to the throne deploring such activities by the wives of officials. He asked the king to rectify this immoral situation by prohibiting women from visiting families other than their parents, siblings, and paternal and maternal uncles.[16] This indeed was the beginning of the severe limitations on women's freedom during the Chosŏn dynasty.

Women's life during the Chosŏn dynasty

In 1915, the Japanese colonial government issued a notice, now recorded in the civil register, to the officials in charge not to receive any petitions from women wanting to establish households apart from their families. This notice was written in the civil register case regulations. Such legal provision does not appear in the Chosŏn National Code (*Kyŏngguk Taejŏn*),[17] but the Japanese colonial government issued a decree that in laws concerning matters of family relationship or inheritance, it would simply follow traditional Korean social customs.[18] It seems that the Chosŏn National Code did not mention such matters because, in the mind of the Chosŏn ruling elite class, women's legal rights were not even worth mentioning.

In the National Code, it is clearly stated that the *yangban* class of women were prohibited from having picnics in the open air, in the mountains, or within the city walls, and those who violated this provision would be punished by one hundred strokes of flogging. In the fourth year of the reign of King Taejong (1406), women were prohibited from visiting Buddhist temples.[19] The only social and official recognition a woman was accorded came through the official position of her husband. The National Code provides a detailed list of positions and titles for the wives of high officials. The collective terms for such titles are *naemyŏngbu* (interior appointed women) for the royal seraglios and *woemyŏngbu* (exterior appointed women) for the wives of the high officials.[20] The National Code also makes it clear that such a title would be forfeited if the woman remarried after the death of her husband.

In day-to-day life, the actual physical area of a woman's activity was nearly confined to her home, especially to the inner court of the household. The so-called *naeoepŏp*, or the code of ethics between male and female, according to which the woman was not supposed to see men other than her own immediate family members, dictated that the woman stay in the inner court or more specifically in her own room called *anbang* or *naesil* (literally, inner room). Without the permission of her husband, she was not allowed to go out of the house. When she went out, she had to ride in a covered palanquin in order not to be seen by other men.[21]

Regardless of class, women were required to cover their faces. In the case of upper-class women, a hat and veil combination called *nŏul* was used to cover the face and head, while lower-class women wore a longer cloth called *chang'ot* to cover themselves from the head down. Women on an outing wearing *chang'ot* are often portrayed in the genre paintings of the late Chosŏn period. Upper-class women never appeared in genre paintings. Lower-class women were also less strictly confined to their homes as they often accompanied their husbands to work in the fields.

This strict code of ethics is reflected in the structure of Korean residential architecture, which separates the living quarters of the master and the matron of the house. When entering the house through the main gate, one faces an outer courtyard surrounded by rooms of the men's quarter called *sarang-ch'ae*. At one corner of this outer court is the middle gate which leads to the inner courtyard. Hallways and rooms, including the kitchen along the courtyard, form the women's quarter *called anch'ae* and the matron's room, *anbang* or *naesil*, is situated in its innermost section, diagonally opposite the middle gate.[22] The men's quarter was absolutely off-limits to female members of the family while the close male members of the family such as masters of the house or brothers of the matron could occasionally enter the matron's room. Consequently, the matron and her daughters had extemely limited contact with outsiders.

Women received no formal education of any sort in traditional Korea.[23] Intelligent girls of the scholar-official families were taught reading and writing by either their grandfather or father, or often a girl would learn to read 'over-the-shoulder' of her brother when he was tutored at home. Traditionally, painting, calligraphy, and poetry were considered requisite activities for cultivated gentlemen. However, women of upper-class families were actively discouraged from cultivating their talents in these arts, in part because official entertainers called *kinyŏ*, usually of lower-class origin, were trained in these arts to perform in the company of men. The sixteenth century *Book of admonition to women of the inner court*, attributed to the famous neo-Confucian philosopher Yi Hwang (1501-1570), outlined what was expected of the upper-class ladies:

> Ladies should be able to compose poems, do calligraphy, read the History, Lesser Learning, and the Admonition to Ladies, and be able to recognise the names of kings and ancestors. However, excessive skill in writing or brilliancy in poetry is rather like *kinyŏ*, and not what is expected of well-born ladies.[24]

Considering such restrictions as those described above, several women of the Chosŏn period who left literary works or paintings and calligraphy of high standard must have been truly exceptional. About seventeen women during the 500 years of the Chosŏn dynasty were recorded to have excelled in painting and calligraphy, but only five of them have surviving works attributed to them: Madam Sin (Sin Saimdang, 1504-1551); her daughter, Madam Yi (Yi Maech' ang, 1529-1592); and her granddaughter,also known as Madam Yi (Pyoggo Puin, 1584-1609); Hŏ Nansŏlhŏn (1563-1589); and Chukhyang (nineteenth century).[25] The first four women were from scholar-officials' families while Chukhyang was a *kinyŏ*.

One common factor noticeable in the poems and paintings of Chosŏn women is the focus on the writers immediate surroundings. Landscape paintings, the most popular and traditionally considered the highest in the hierarchy of themes since the Northern Song dynasty, were seldom executed by women as they had little opportunity to experience the grandeur and wonders of nature first-hand. The majority of paintings attributed to Sin Saimdang are of subjects she could easily observe from her courtyard-small birds, flowers, insects or 'the Four Gentlemen' (plum, orchid, chrysanthemum and bamboo) in ink, another traditional theme of literati painting. She left only a few small landscapes.[26] The same is true of her daughter and granddaughter.

Outdoor themes are equally rare in the work of Hŏ Nansŏlhŏn, better known as a poet than a painter. In her *Collected poems* one occasionally finds titles such as 'Lotus Pond' and 'Moon-night', subjects she could ponder in her own secluded living quarters. There are occasional exceptions like 'On the River Bank' or the 'Dream journey to the Kwang-san mountains', but the latter is clearly based on her imagination rather than her experience.[27] The vast majority of her poems, however, portray her inner world of sorrow and agony.[28]

Like Sin Saimdang, the nineteenth-century courtesan Chukhyang also painted flowers and insects. She is recorded to have executed ink bamboo paintings which were highly praised by the scholar painter, Sin Wi (1769-1845), himself a most prominent ink bamboo painter of the late Chosŏn period. In his colophon to Chukhyang'sink bamboo painting, which he labeled as 'a bundle of fragrance', Sin Wi stated that she had modeled her ink bamboo after his own.[29]

Of these five women artists, Sin Saimdang is the most well known and also is one to whom the largest number of paintings are attributed. What makes her so famous, however, is not her artistic output, but the fact that she is the mother of one of the most celebrated neo-Confucian philosophers in Korean history, Yulgok Yi Yi (1536-1584). Saimdang's own father was also a scholar-official of significance, and this accounts for the unusually good education she received from her father and grandfather.[30] In Korean history, she is revered as a model of *hyŏnmo yangch'ŏ,* or a wise mother and a good wife.[31]

The paintings attributed to Saimdang vary widely in quality and style. The fact that she was the mother of the celebrated neo-Confucian scholar seems to be rather detrimental to the fair evaluation of her work as a painter. Many of these painting have colophons written by rather well-known scholar-officials of the seventeenth and eighteenth century, most of them followers of the seventeenth century neo-Confucian philosopher, Song Si-yŏl (1607-1698), who is no other than the principal follower of Saimdang's son, Yi Yulgok. In fact, Song Si-yŏl was the first to identify Saimdang as an excellent painter of grass and insects[32] and it is likely that after Song Si-yŏl's time, many grass-and-insect paintings of questionable merit were attributed to her.

Saimdang was also praised for her talent in embroidery. An embroidered screen of eight panels attributed to her is now kept in the Tong-a University Museum in Pusan, the southern port city. Embroidered on black silk, the centrally placed flowers with butterflies and insects around them, a widely used pattern in the late Chosŏn period, resembles many of the grass-and-insect paintings attributed to her.

The case of Hŏ Nansŏlhŏn was also interesting in that it was her brother, Hŏ Kyun (1569-1618), who was instrumental in recognising and promoting his sister's literary and artistic talent. In fact, Hŏ Kyun himself was one of the most well-known literary figures of the time; his novel, *Hong Kiltongjŏn* (The Story of Hong Kiltong) is a classic of Korean literature. Nansŏlhŏn's husband, Kim Song-rip (1562-1592), was also a scholar and poet of some renown, a circumstance that enabled her to cultivate her talent in literature and art. With the help of her brother, she was able to leave to posterity a collection of her poems in one volume.[33] There are a handful of paintings attributed to her, but only a small landscape with a figure called 'Looking at the Flying Birds', which has been transmitted from generation to generation to the present owner, the twelfth generation descendant of Hŏ Hwa (Nansŏlhŏn's father) is likely to be hers.[34]

The nineteenth-century courtesan Chukhyang gained fame as a talented painter of flowers and ink bamboo through the support of the scholar-official Sin Wi, whom she served. Despite her mean origin, Chukhyang's talent and job enabled her to communicate with a highly sophisticated gentleman such as Sin Wi and share with him her creative output. Needless to say, Chukhyang is one in a thousand among the courtesans of the

Chosŏn period who had the good fortune of being recognised and recorded in the collected works of a contemporary literatus. Interestingly, the proscriptive provisions of the Penal Code of the National Code clearly states that courtesans were the only exceptions in the proscription of lavishness in costumes and accessories of women. Another exceptional 'privilege' they enjoyed, out of necessity in carrying out their job, was the exemption from the strict *naeoepŏp* , or the code of ethics of gender separation.[35]

Conclusion

Korean women of the Chosŏn dynasty were subjected to severe restrictions in all aspects of daily life. Their physical domain of life was, in most cases, confined to the inner quarter of their homes. Under no circumstances were they given formal education, and they were not allowed to have any contact with men other than the immediate members of their family. Despite such restrictions, some tried and succeeded in fulfilling their intellectual and artistic potential. While Sin Saimdang and Hŏ Nansŏlhŏn of the sixteenth century were women of scholar-gentry families who became well known primarily because they were the mother or the sister of leading figures of the period, Chukhyang in the nineteenth century was a woman of lower birth who made her fame through her own talent and her more direct contact with contemporary gentlemen artists, a privilege which she enjoyed because of her courtesan status. Although the number of women painters or poets who made their way into history during the five centuries of the Chosŏn dynasty is almost insignificant, their mere existence is quite important in the social and cultural history of pre-modern Korea.

Needlecrafts were practiced by all classes of women. Lowerclass women servants who produced needlecrafts for the court left their names in the documents of the Chosŏn dynasty's royal weddings.[36] But they are just names without any social context except their approximate date of activity. There is no way to match these names with the existing embroidery works or the wrapping cloths. Therefore, with a few exceptions, almost all the needlework remains anonymous, yet it represents the highest artistic sensibility of traditional Korea.

Yi Sŏng-mi is Professor of Art History, The Academy of Korean Studies, Songnam-si, Korea

Notes

1. The pioneering work on the subject of Korean women is Yi Nung-hwa, *Chosŏn Yŏsokko* (Customs of Chosŏn women), first published in 1926. A more comprehensive modern work, *Han'guk Yŏsŏngsa* (History of Korean women) is a collection of essays published in 1972 by Ehwa Women's University. The abridged version of this work was published in English as *Women of Korea: a history from ancient times to 1945* (edited and translated by Yung-Chung Kim), also published by Ehwa Women's University in 1975. A nine-volume compilation of historical documents and literary works on women was also published by Ehwa Women's University in 1981, under the title of *Han'guk Yŏsŏng Kwan'gye Charyojip* (Collection of sources on Korean women).
2. Both the hallowed-and true-bone ranks are of the Kim clan, one of the founding families of the Silla Kingdom. Although it is not entirely clear what distinguishes the two ranks, the division seems to have been decided on the basis of the maternal lineage. See Ki-baik Lee, *A new history of Korea,* translated by Edward W Wagner with Edward J Shultz, Ilchogak, Seoul, 1984, pp 49-50.
3. Kim Pu-sik, *Samguk Sagi* (History of the Three Kingdoms), vol 5, Queen Sŏndŏk, quoted in *Women of Korea, op cit,* p 27. When she was young, the court of China's Tang dynasty sent gifts of peony seeds and paintings of peony flowers which were greatly admired. But the young princess noticed that there were no butterflies and bees around the flowers in the paintings and said, 'These flowers have no fragrance. What a pity!' Indeed when the seeds wereplanted and the flowers bloomed, the flowers had no fragrance.
4. *Women of Korea*, p 39.
5. See p 24
6. 'Princess Sŏnhwa, / Hoping for a secret marriage, / Went away at night, / With Mattung (later King Mu) in her arms.' From Peter Lee, *Poems from Korea,* Honolulu, 1974, quoted in *Women of Korea*, p 66.
7. 'Having caroused far into the night, / In the Moonlit capital, / I returned home and in my bed, / Behold, four legs, Two have been mine; / Whose are the other two? / Two had been mine; / No, no, they are taken.' *Ibid,* p 67.
8. Yi, Hak, *Hansu Munhwa* (The culture of Korean embroidery), Seoul, 1986, p 203.
9. *Ibid.*

10. 'Pulguksa kogŭm ch'anggi' (History of the Pulguksa Temple), quoted in *ibid*, p 204.
11. *Han'guk Yŏsŏngsa, op cit*, p 223. Also see the recent book by Martina Deuchler, *Confucian transformation of Korea*, Harvard University Press, Cambridge, 1992, pp 51-6 for cases of property division during the Koryŏ period.
12. Deuchler, *op cit*, p 56.
13. *Hanguk ŭi Yŏinsang* (Images of Korean women), Ministry of Health and Social Affairs, Korea (ed),Seoul, 1971, p 95.
14. *Ibid*, p 94.
15. *Koryŏsa* (History of the Koryŏ dynasty), *kwon* 56, Biography of Sin Wu in annotated *Koryŏsa* (10 vols), vol 4, (Tong-a University, 1987), p 284.
16. *Veritable Record of King T'aejo*, vol 1, entry from day *kihae*,Sept 1393, quoted in *Han'guk Yŏsŏngsa*, p 447.
17. *Kyŏngguk Taejŏn* (National Code) in six volumes (in Chinese) is the basic National Code of the Chosŏn dynasty compiled by the order of King Sejo (reign 1456-1468) which covers all aspects of national affairs. It was revised four times between 1470-1485. The annotated Korean translation of the Code by Han U-gŭn, Yi Sŏng-mu and others was published by the Academy of Korean Studies in 1985.
18. *Han'guk Yŏsŏngsa*, p 474. However, since the enactment of the Civil Law in 1960, Korean women today can legally become the head of a household. See Article No. 788 of the Civil Law. Yi Hyo-jae and Kim Chu-suk, *Hanguk Yŏsŏng ŭi Chiwi* (The status of Korean women), Ehwa Women's University Press, 1976, p 54.
19. The annotated and translated version of the National Code, *op cit*, vol 5, Penal Code, Proscriptive Provisions, pp 440-441.
20. *Ibid*, vol 1, Personnel Code, pp 4-6.
21. *Chosŏn Yŏsokko, op cit*, p 234.
22. The Kim family residence in Waryong-dong in Seoul is a typical example of such a house built in 1750. See the plan of the house in Chu Nam-chole, *Han'guk ŭi Chutaek Kŏn-ch'uk* (Korean Residential Architecture), Ilchi-sa, Seoul, 1980, p 90, fig 38.
23. The first educational institution for women in Korea was established in 1886 by the American missionary, Madam Scranton. The school called Ehwa Hakdang opened its door with only one student, but fifteen years later, in 1901, there were 174 students, and in 1910, the college division was established. See Yi Hyo-jae and Kim Chu-suk, *op cit*, p 85. Later, Ehwa Hakdang developed into a prestigious six-year girls' school which consisted of a three-year middle and a three-year high school. It now exists as a three-year girls' high school called Ehwa Girls' High School. Its college division, the present Ehwa Women's University, is now the largest women's university in the world with an enrollment of nearly 20,000 students.
24. *Kyujung Yoram* (The book of admonition to women of the inner court), attributed to Yi Hwang, quoted in the *Han'guk Yŏsŏngsa*, p 572.
25. In Yi Sŏng-mi, 'Chosŏn Sidae Yŏryu Hwaga Yŏn'gu' (Women painters of the Chosŏn dynasty), in *Misul Charyo* (Art materials), no 51 (The National Museum of Korea, June 1993), pp 98-149. Paintings of Madam Sin, Maech'ang, and Pyŏggo Puin are discussed. An English abstract of the article can be found in *ibid*, pp 167-170.
26. See the list of works attributed to Sin Saimdang in Yi Sŏng-mi, *op cit*, pp 148-149.
27. *Hŏ Nansŏlhŏn Sijip* (Collected poems of Hŏ Nansŏlhŏn), annotated and translated into Korean by O Hae-in, Haein Munhwasa, Seoul, 1980, pp 155, 185, 284, and 190ff.
28. For example, see, Kichung Kim, 'Chosŏn dynasty women seen through their own eyes's, *Profusion of colour: Korean costumes and wrapping cloths of the Chosŏn dynasty*, Asian Art Museum of San Fransisco, 1995, pp 17-24.
29. *Kyŏngsudang Chŏngo* (Complete works of Sin Wi), quoted in O Se-ch'ang, *Kŭnyŏk Sŏhwajing* (Biographical dictionary of Korean painters and calligraphers), 1917, p 238.
30. The most comprehensive biographies of Saimdang and her family members can be found in Yi Ŭn-sang, *Saimdang ŭi Saeng'aewa Yesul* (Life and art of Saimdang), Songmuk-gak, Seoul, 1982, revised edition.
31. Her position in the history of Korean women is well demonstrated by the Saimdang Award which has been given to the best wife and mother of the year by the Korean Association of Housewives since 1969.
32. See the list of writers of colophons to Sin Saimdang'paintings in Yi Sŏng-mi, *op cit*, pp 136-137. In this list, there are twenty-two writers in chronological order from the sixteenth century to the twentieth century. Of these, ten fall in the period between the mid seventeenth century and the end of the eighteenth century. Amidst the factional strife of the Chosŏn court, Song Si-yŏl for a while fell into disfavour, but was soon reinstated at the end of the seventeenth century, and numerous neo-Confucian academies honoring him were established during eighteenth century.
33. For Nansŏlhŏn's literary achievement, see Mun Kyŏng-hyŏn, *Hŏ Nansŏlhŏn Chonjip* (Collected work of Hŏ Nansŏlhŏn), Seoul, 1972.
34. Other works which carry traditional attribution to her are the 'Pasturing Horses' and the 'Peonies', both of which are in the National Museum of Korea, Seoul. They strongly display styles of paintings of the eighteenth century or later.
35. Kim Yong-suk, *Hanguk Yŏsoksa* (A history of the customs of Korean women), Minŭmsa, Seoul, 1980, p 253.

36. Since 1627, there were twenty cases of royal weddings (kings and crown princes) during the Chosŏn dynasty which remain today in the form of handwritten books. These are the detailed records of all stages of the event along with the names of persons who participated in the event in various capacities, and therefore, they provide us with a mine of information on the culture of the period. See Yi Sŏng-mi, et al, *Changsŏgak Sojang Karye Togam Ŭigwe* (Records of the Superintendency of the Royal Weddings in the Changsŏgak Library), The Academy of Korean Studies, 1994, for more on the records and their art historical and cultural significances.

Then and now : the cultural meanings and design of Korean costume and wrapping cloths

Min-Jung Kim

In the West, Korea has often been thought of as little more than a cultural bridge between China and Japan. Contrary to this misconception, however, Korean art and culture is both distinctive and unique. Whilst historically China has exerted a strong influence on Korean culture, much of this influence has been modified by a Korean aesthetic sensibility which has its origins in Korean history and the natural environment. For example, the typical arrangement of five striped colours seen in the sleeves of many Korean costumes and wrapping cloths derives from the Chinese philosophy of *yin* and *yang* and the five elements known in Korean as *Eumyangohang* (literally negative and positive and the five directions). This is an East Asian cosmology which explains the principle of creation and destruction within the universe. *Eum* and *yang* represent the harmony of opposites such as the moon and the sun, cold and warm, woman and man, shade and sun, and *Ohang* refers to the four directions and centre of a compass. Each of the five directions is accorded a colour. For example blue represents west, white represents east, red represents south, black represents north and yellow the centre. These colours are lighter in tone than the original Chinese five-colours.

In a classical Chinese text there is a reference to Koreans as 'eastern foreigners who enjoy singing and dancing'[1] which alludes to cultural distinctions between the two peoples and may in part explain why the colours adopted by Korean people are lighter and brighter in tone than those used by the Chinese. The use of colour in Korean costumes and wrapping cloths derives from the *Eumyangohang* philosophy and people's belief that the conscious composition of these colours will bring good luck and prevent evil.

The creators of the costume and textiles in this exhibition were anonymous women whose lives were affected by the strict social ideology of the Chosŏn dynasty (1392-1910). Within a social hierarchy which privileged men, women found enjoyment through needlework as sewing and embroidery were among the few accepted or encouraged activities through which they could explore their talent. Hand-sewn clothing and functional textiles such as wrapping cloths from the Chosŏn period are therefore a poignant expression of the way in which Korean women entertained themselves and communicated their passion, love and hope.

Traditional dress for Korean men and women is a two-piece ensemble. Men wore trousers (*paji*) and a jacket (*chŏgori*) and women a skirt (*chi'ma*) and jacket (*chŏgori*) which together are known as the basic *hanbok*. The design of these garments derives from north Asian nomadic culture. This two piece design was more practical in cold weather and was suited to a nomadic lifestyle.[2] Formal court dress, however comprised a one piece robe which originated from China. This was also worn by the upper class as formal dress. Two distinct systems of dress – one Korean and one Chinese – were therefore used concurrently in Korea. However, the basic *hanbok* was worn under the Chinese style court robe and was also worn as a home dress and night gown.

Yellow jackets and red skirts were usually worn by unmarried women. They were also worn under the bridal robe. To avoid the uniformity of the standard cut of the the jacket, contrasting coloured material was applied to the collar (*git*), tie (*goreum*), sleeve cuffs (*keutdong*) and armpit insertions (*giyutmagi*). These coloured additions embellished the simplicity of the jacket's design and added a refreshing colour harmony. At the same time they represented the social status of the wearer, as only upper class women were allowed to wear jackets with armpit insertions. The jacket was also designed to accommodate easy laundering. A narrow white neckband known as *dongjung*, which had direct contact with the neck, was lined with paper and stitched over the collar. The neck-liner could be easily removed when it became dirty thus economising on cleaning and unnecessary expense. When an entire garment required cleaning, women would unpick all of the seams and wash the fabric sections by hand. The fabric lengths were then ironed and restiched with new thread. Sometimes, after many years of wear the fabric would be reversed for better colour and renewed strength. And eventually, after further wear and tear the garments would be cut up and recycled into patchwork wrapping cloths.

Korean women favoured long and wide skirts with many pleats hence the custom of fastening the skirt above the breast rather than around the waist. This accentuated the long triangular line of the skirt which was further heightened by the progressive shortening of the jacket or *chŏgori* during the seventeenth, eighteenth and nineteenth centuries. The width of a skirt determined a wearer's status. Measurement was made by the unit *p'ok* (approximately 35cm). For example a skirt could be 6 *p'ok*, 12 *p'ok* or13 *p'ok* in width. The skirt was stiched to a straight waist band, wrapped around the body and fastened at the back. The way of wrapping determined the status of the wearer. Upper class women wrapped the skirt to the left and lower class women and entertainment girls (*kinyŏ*) wrapped it to the right. Trousers and slips were worn underneath the skirts.

The women's robe known as *wŏnsam* was introduced from China to Korea during the United Silla period (AD 668-935). It was originally worn as a semi-formal robe at court and as a formal robe by upper class women. During the later part of the Chosŏn dynasty it was worn by ordinary people as a wedding robe. The sleeves were originally composed of two colours-red and yellow or red and blue. *Wŏnsam* worn at court had two-colour sleeves whereas *wŏnsam* worn by ordinary people had five-colour striped sleeves.[3] This was because the majority of Korean people preferred to use colours based on the *Eumyangohang* philosophy. To further highlight the influence of this philosophy on Korean dress a contrasting colour was used for the lining of the robe to symbolise *eum* and *yang*. Chinese characters meaning longevity (*su*) and good fortune(*pok*) were often printed in gold on a long belt which fastened at the back of the robe. The sides of robe were split so that when it was worn over the skirt (*ch'ima*) and jacket (*chŏgori*), the side panels would fan out and create a silhouette that was broader and longer than the actual shape of the *wŏnsam*. The sleeves were designed to be much longer than the length of the arm, as it was a courtesy not to show the hands during formal meetings when the *wŏnsam* was worn.

Another robe that was introduced from China around same period as the *wŏnsam* is the 'flower robe' known as *hwarrot*. Like the *wŏnsam*, this robe was also worn over the skirt (*ch'ima*) and jacket (*chŏgori*) and created a similar silhouette. It was originally worn as a wedding dress at court but during the late Chosŏn period it was also worn by ordinary people as a wedding dress. The robe is tied with a belt decorated with a phoenix motif known as *pongti*. The phoenix symbolises royalty and in particular the queen. Embroidered auspicious motifs which often appear on the *hwarrot* are the peony, lotus, butterfly, waves, cloud, rock, *pullocho* (herb for eternal youth), crane, phoenix and children. Together these motifs symbolise the feminine, love, fertility, longevity and happiness in life. Chinese characters are embroidered on the front and back of the robe and convey the meaning of marriage. Chinese script was embroidered on wedding garments in preference to Korean characters because Chinese culture was held in high regard and the incorporation of Chinese text was regarded as a sign of cultivation. The Korean language known as *Hangŭl*, that is now in common use and used in preference to Chinese language, was created by King Saejong in 1446. Women and lower class people were permitted to learn *Hangŭl* whereas Chinese was restricted to the upper class. During the Chosŏn dynasty however, the use of Korean characters was generally shunned by the intelligentsia and the upper class whereas Korean characters were used by many women and lower class people. *Hangŭl* being a phonetically based language was also much easier to learn than Chinese.

Another form of women's court dress that is believed to have originated in China is the jacket known as *tang'ui* or Tang-style robe. The *tang'ui* was worn together with a red or indigo skirt (*ch'ima*). The Queen and royal concubines of the Chosŏn dynasty wore the *tang'ui* as semi-formal dress, whereas and high-ranking court ladies and upper-class ladies wore it as formal dress. The most common colour of *tang'ui* was green. Red was restricted to use by the Queen. Even though there were different colours of *tang'ui*, the ties were always a reddish-purple colour and the garment was lined with pink silk and the cuffs were lined with white fabric stiffened with paper.[4] The distinctive feature of the *tang'ui* is its shape. The jacket comprises narrow front and back panels which kick up at the bottom. This upwarding curving shape can also be found in the upturned toe of Korean socks, the corner of the woman's jacket (*chŏgori*) which fastens with the bow tie and in the roofline of traditional Korean buildings.

In Korea today traditional-style dress is still popularly worn by men, women and children on special occasions. For example children wear *hanbok* on their first birthday and on lunar festival days such as New Year and the Moon Festival. It is also common for married women to wear *hanbok* when they attend important ceremonies such as the wedding of family members, formal parties and sixtieth birthday celebrations. A young bride would generally wear a Western-style white wedding dress and after the ceremony change into a traditional traditional Korean *wŏnsam or hwarrot* for the formal greeting between the bride and the grooms family (*p'aebaek*). It is also common practice for people to prepare garments for the after life known as *sueui* and for family members attending a funeral to wear white *hanbok*.

Wrapping cloths known as *pojagi* are familiar items of daily use in Korean society. Traditionally they were made by women from all classes of society. They are square or rectangular cloths that were used to cover food and wrap clothing, bedding, gifts and other precious items. The Korean word *potari santa* meaning 'to pack' may be literally translated as 'wrapping luggage with a wrapping cloth'. Wrapping cloths may be embroidered, painted, made from oiled paper, patchwork or just plain cloth. The earliest recorded use of *pojagi* is in the legend of the founding of the Kaya Kingdom in AD 42. Legend has it that the King of Kaya was born from a golden egg contained within golden box sent from the heaven which was wrapped with a red *pojagi*.[5] In addition to being used for practical purposes, *pojagi* also indicated the status of the wrapped articles, the wishes of the maker and respect which was conveyed by the act of wrapping.

As a result of Westernisation and modernisation, Korean life styles have changed dramatically since the *Chosŏn* period. While many wrapping cloths have been replaced by Western-style shopping bags and handbags, they are still used to wrap important documents in the National Assembly and they are an important item that must be prepared for the wedding ceremony. Most contemporary wrapping cloths used for such purposes are commercial products which preserve the form and meaning of the tradition, though not its original beauty. When visiting markets in Korea, it is also possible to see elderly women carrying goods wrapped with wrapping cloths skillfully balanced on their head. For the younger generation however, the experience of using wrapping cloths may only be carrying a warm lunchbox to school in a wrapping cloth-but that is only if they could not convince their mother to buy a Western-style bag, because wrapping cloths are now considered by many young people to be old fashioned. Interestingly however, wrapping cloths have found new ways of surviving within contemporary Korean society. Wrapping cloths are frequently used to carry purchases made from dress or *hanbok* shops, advertising the skill of their makers and some have even become art objects created by professional crafts people who specialise in their making. Contemporary makers however do not automatically practice frugality and create works from recycled fabrics which have stories of life to tell. These contemporary makers cannot ignore the legacy of past Korean women who created objects which were highly functional, but ultimately of great and lasting beauty.

Min-Jung Kim is assistant curator at the Powerhouse Museum, Sydney

Notes

1. Jinsu (AD 233-297), *Samkukji* (History of Three Kingdoms) (AD 220-280), *Wiji* Record of Wi Country, *Dongeuicheun*, China (Korean chapter).
2. Suk Joo-Sun, *Hankukpoksik ui Pyŏnchŏn* (Evolution of Korean costumes), *Han'guk ui Mi* (Beauty of Korea: traditional costumes, ornaments and wrappings cloth), exhibition catalogue, National Museum of Korea, Seoul, 1988, p 117.
3. Suk Joo-Sun, *Hankukpoksik ui Pyŏnchŏn* (Evolution of Korean costumes), *Han'guk ui Mi* (Beauty of Korea: traditional costumes, ornaments and wrappings cloth), exhibition catalogue, National Museum of Korea, Seoul, 1988, p 128.

4. Lee Sun-Jae and others, *Han'guk Misul Munwhaui Yihae* (Understanding Korean art and culture), *Doseochulpan Yehkyŏng*, 1994, p 339.
5. Publishing Committee of Dictionary of Korean Myths and Symbols, *Dictionary of Korean myths and symbols* (Han'guk Mumwha Sangjin Sacheon), Dong-A Publishing & Printing Co Ltd, Seoul, 1992, p 345.

Korean textiles and costumes
of the Chosŏn dynasty

1. Wŏnsam (bridal robe), silk *(tan)* with self-patterned design, green, red, blue, yellow, pink and white, 19th century, (220cm, 122cm).

1. Wŏnsam (bridal robe), silk *(tan)* with self-patterned design, green, red, blue, yellow, pink and white, 19th century, (220cm, 122cm).

2. Hwarrot (bridal robe), silk *(tan)* embroidered with floral, bird and character design, red, blue, yellow, pink and white, 18th century, (113cm, 146cm).

2. Hwarrot (bridal robe), silk *(tan)* embroidered with floral, bird and character design, red, blue, yellow, pink and white, 18th century, (113cm, 146cm).

3. Tang'ui (woman's jacket), silk *(tan)* with self patterned peony design, green, white and red, 19th century, (134cm, 84cm).

4. Ch'ima (skirt), silk *(sa)* with self-patterned design, red, 19th century, (114cm, 112cm).

5. Chŏgori (woman's jacket), silk *(sa)* with self-patterned design, yellow and red, 19th century, (26cm, 130cm).

6. a - b Paeja chŏgori (man's jacket and vest), 19th century,
a. Paeja (vest) - silk *(sa)* with self patterned design, green, (62cm, 93cm).
b. Chŏgori (jacket) - silk *(myŏngju)*, purple, (61cm, 58cm).

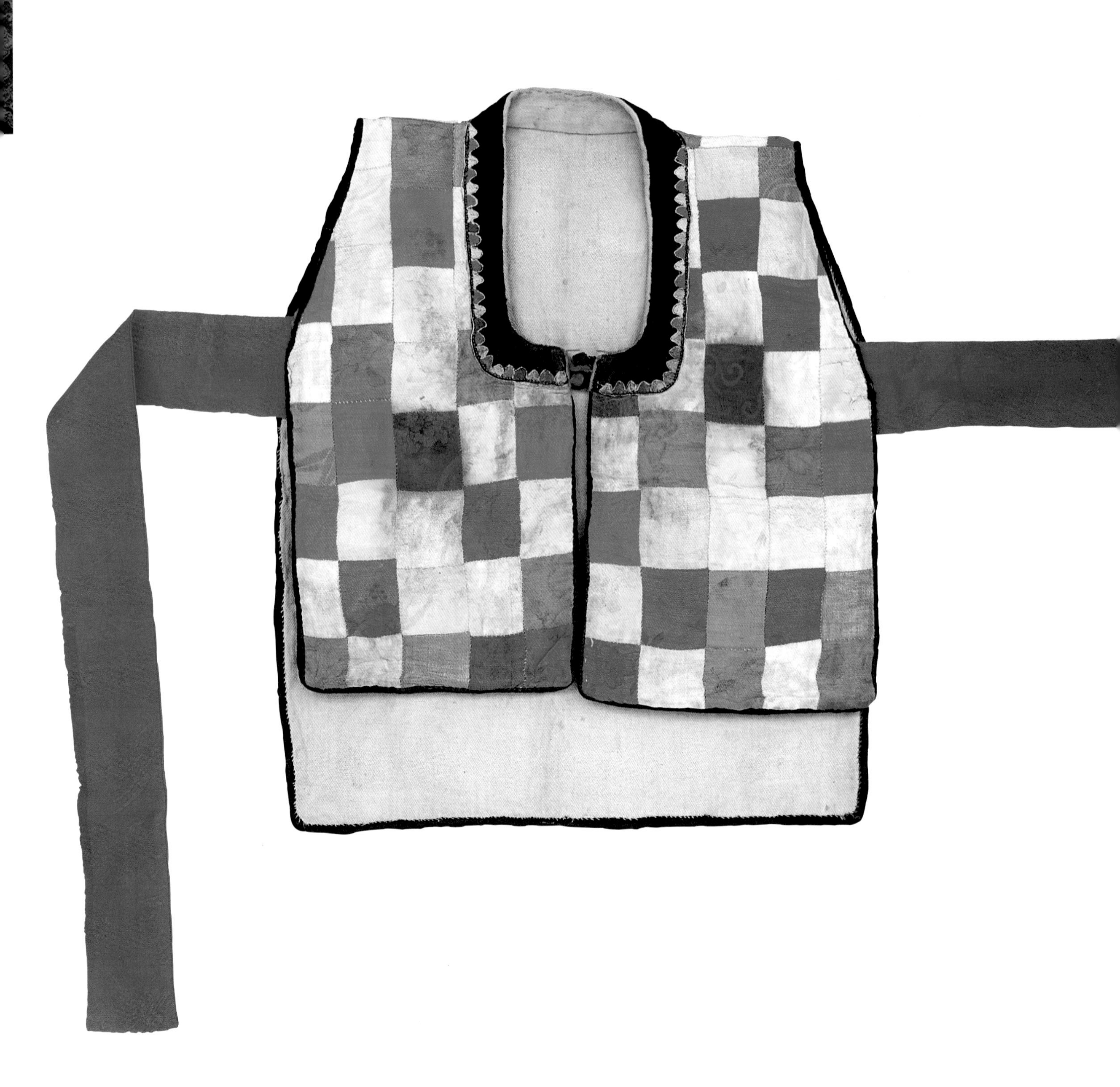

7. Paeja (baby's vest), silk *(sa)* with self-patterned design, red, blue, yellow and black, 19th century, (27cm, 34cm).

8. a-b. Mubok (shaman's robe and long vest), 19th century
a. Robe - silk *(sa)*, green and red, (129cm, 147cm).
b. Long vest - silk *(sa)* , black, (220cm, 122cm).

9. a-d. Chobok (Confucian scholar's ceremonial robe), 19th century
a. *Chŏkch'oui* (red coat), silk *(sa)*, (188cm, 116cm).
b. *Ch'ŏng ch'oui* (blue coat), silk *(sa)*, (146cm, 180cm).
c. *Hunsang* (apron), silk, red, (97cm, 88cm).
d. *Husu* (insignia), silk embroidered with cranes, lotus scrolls, clouds and swastika designs, (11cm, 31.5cm).

9. a-d. Chobok (Confucian scholar's ceremonial robe), 19th century
a. *Chŏkch'oui* (red coat), silk *(sa)*, (188cm, 116cm).
b. *Ch'ŏng ch'oui* (blue coat), silk *(sa)*, (146cm, 180cm).
c. *Hunsang* (apron), silk, red, (97cm, 88cm).
d. *Husu* (insignia), silk embroidered with cranes, lotus scrolls, clouds and swastika designs, (11cm, 31.5cm).

Korean textiles and costumes of the Chosŏn dynasty

10. Princess Myŏng'an's Yedan Po (wrapping cloth for gifts by the bride's family to the groom's family), silk *(tan)* with seven treasures and cloud pattern, blue, 17th century, (107cm, 111cm).

11. Queen's Su Po (embroidered wrapping cloth), silk *(tan)* embroidered with bird and flower design, 17th century, (82cm, 93cm).

12. Yedan Su Po (wrapping cloth for gift for wedding ceremony), silk *(tan)* embroidered with floral decoration, 18th century, (49cm, 49cm).

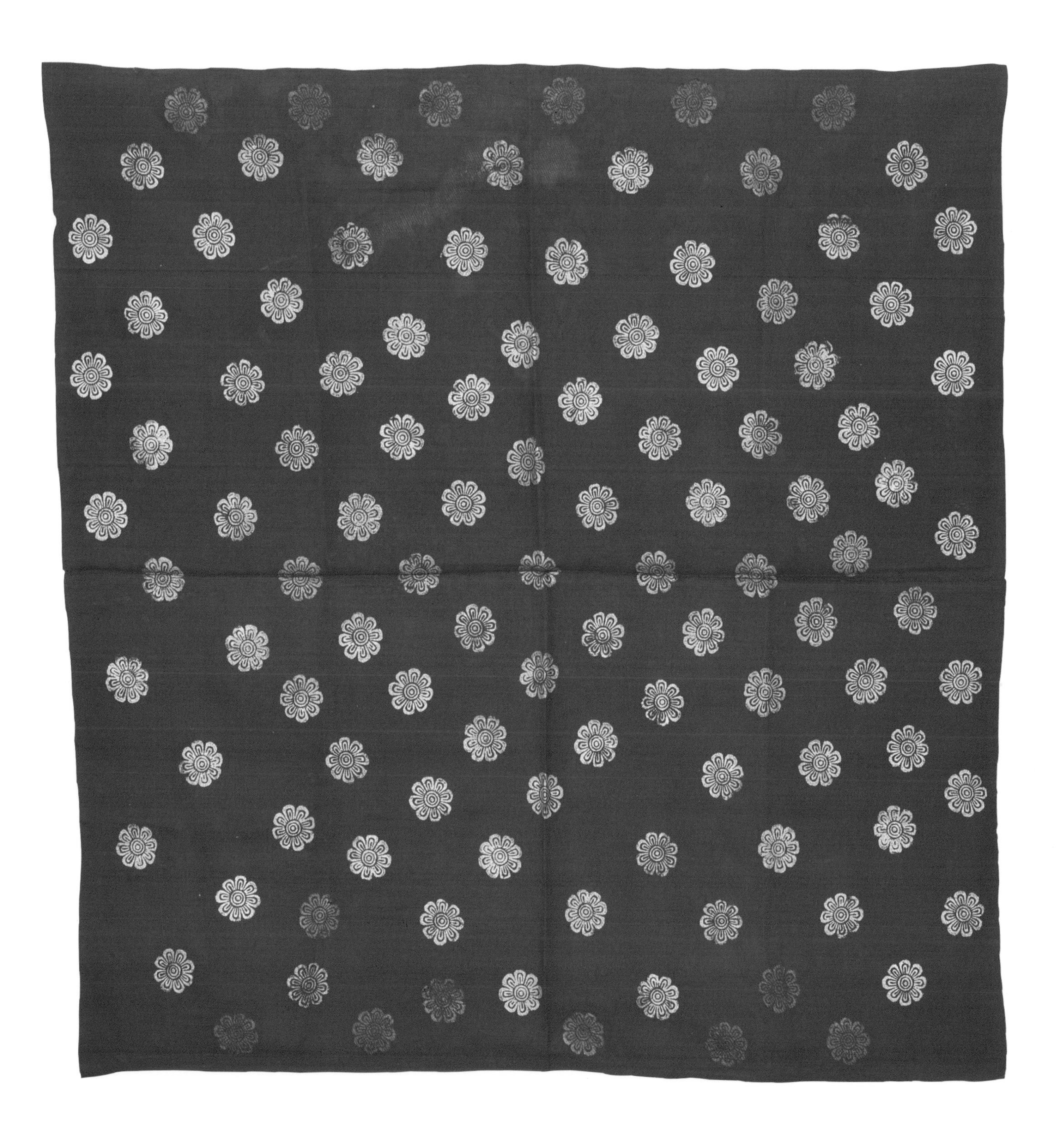

13. Kŭmbak Po (wrapping cloth with gold design), silk *(tan)* with pressed gold design, red, 19th century, (72cm, 72cm).

14. Tangch'ae Po (wrapping cloth with painted design), ramie *(moshi)* painted with confronting phoenixes, floral and other auspicious patterns in red and blue colours, 19th century (70cm, 70cm).

15. Tangch'ae Po (wrapping cloth with painted design), cotton *(myŏn)* painted with auspicious symbols of peonies, cranes, turtles, phoenix and deer, 19th century, (93cm, 93cm).

16. Tangch'ae Po (wrapping cloth with painted design), cotton *(myŏn)* painted with floral and character designs, 19th century, (93cm, 97cm).

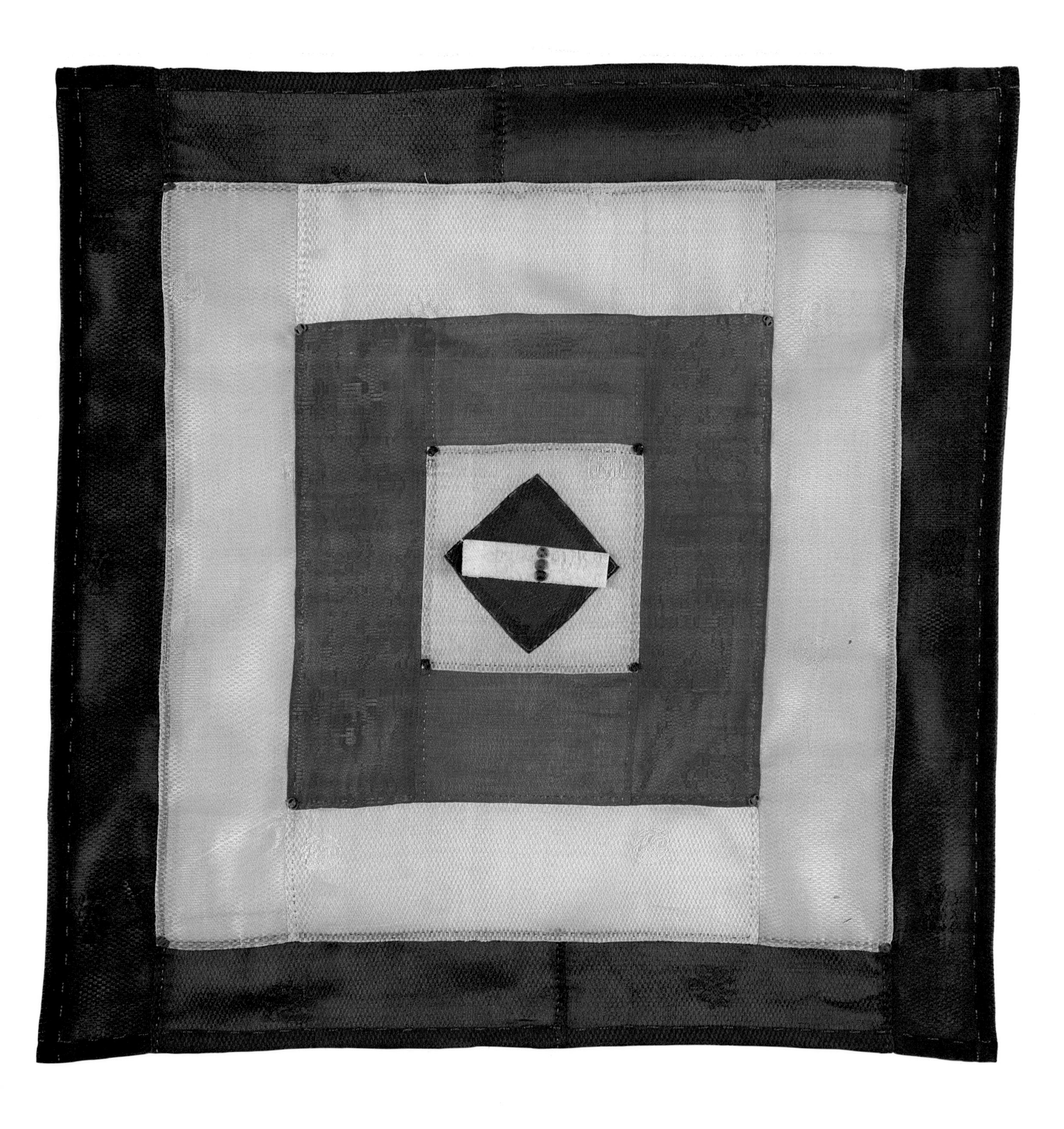

17. Sang Po (wrapping cloth for covering a food table or tray), silk *(sa)* with self-patterned design, unlined, 19th century, 52cm, 52cm).

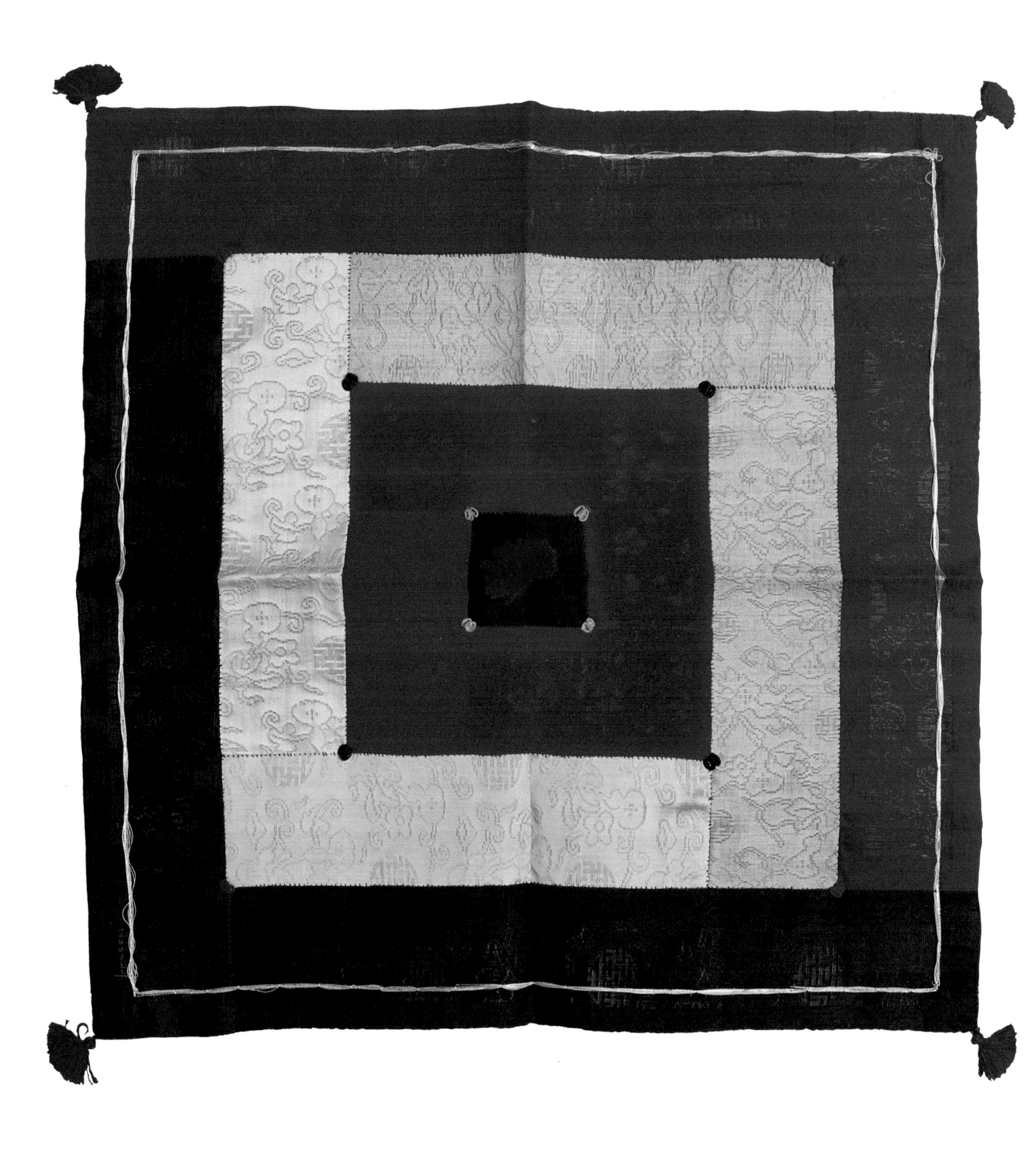

18. Sang Po, silk *(sa)* with self-patterned design, 19th century, (44cm, 44cm).

19. Sang Po, silk *(sa)* with self-patterned design, 19th century, (38cm, 38cm).

20. Sang Po, self - patterned and unpatterned silk *(sa and myŏngju)*, 19th century, (42cm, 42cm).

21. Yuji Sang Po (wrapping cloth lined with oiled paper for covering food), self - patterned silk *(sa)* with patchwork design and lined with oil paper *(yuji)*, 19th century, (49.5cm, 49cm).

22. Sang Po, silk *(sa)* with self-patterned design, 19th century, (48cm,48 cm).

23. Sang Po, silk *(sa)* with self - patterned design, 19th century, (51cm, 50cm).

24. Sang Po, silk *(sa)* with self - patterned design, 19th century, (47cm, 46cm).

25. Sang Po, silk *(sa)* with self - patterned design, 19th century, (48cm, 48cm).

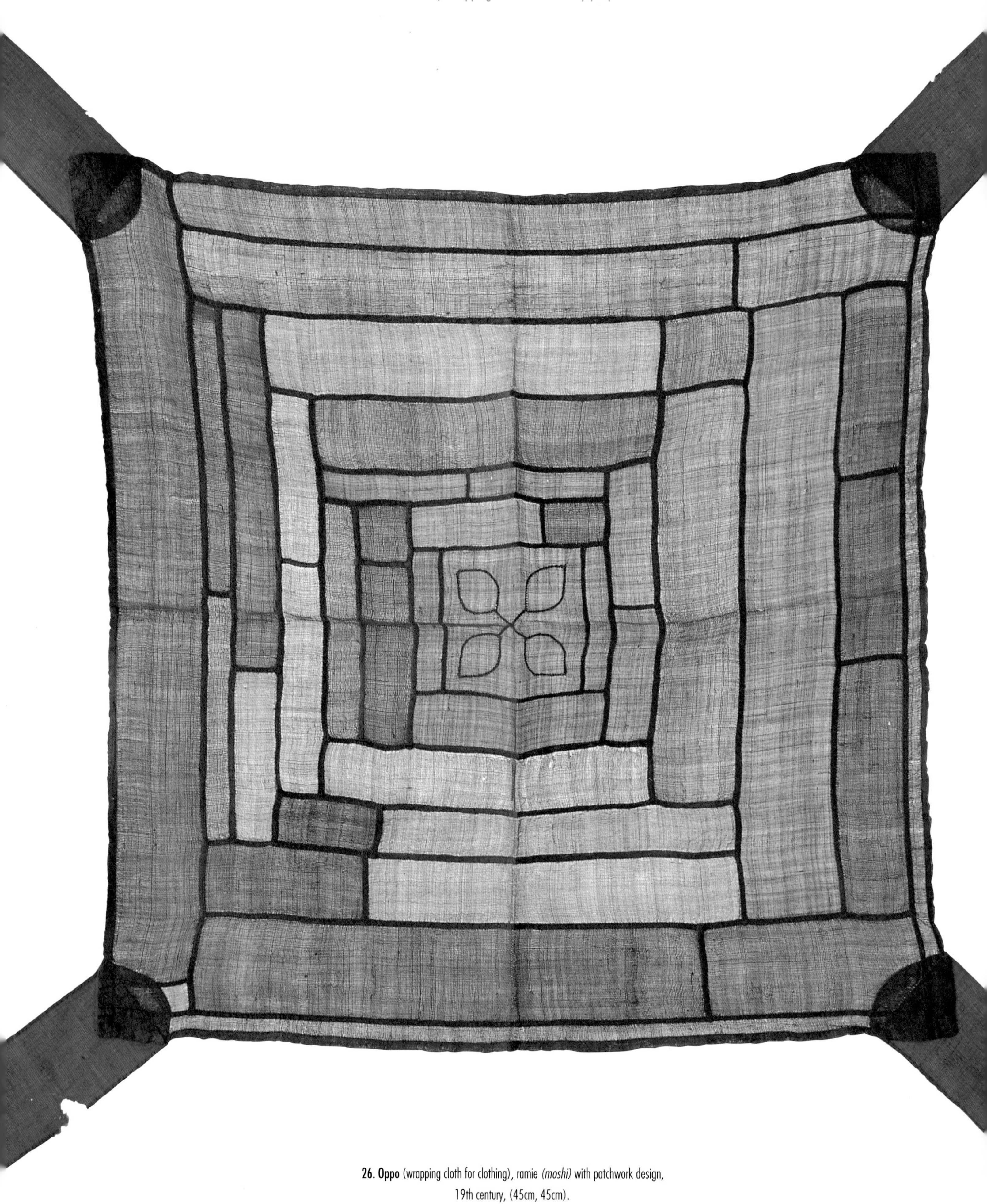

26. Oppo (wrapping cloth for clothing), ramie *(moshi)* with patchwork design, 19th century, (45cm, 45cm).

27. Oppo, ramie *(moshi)* with patchwork design, 19th century, (45cm, 45cm).

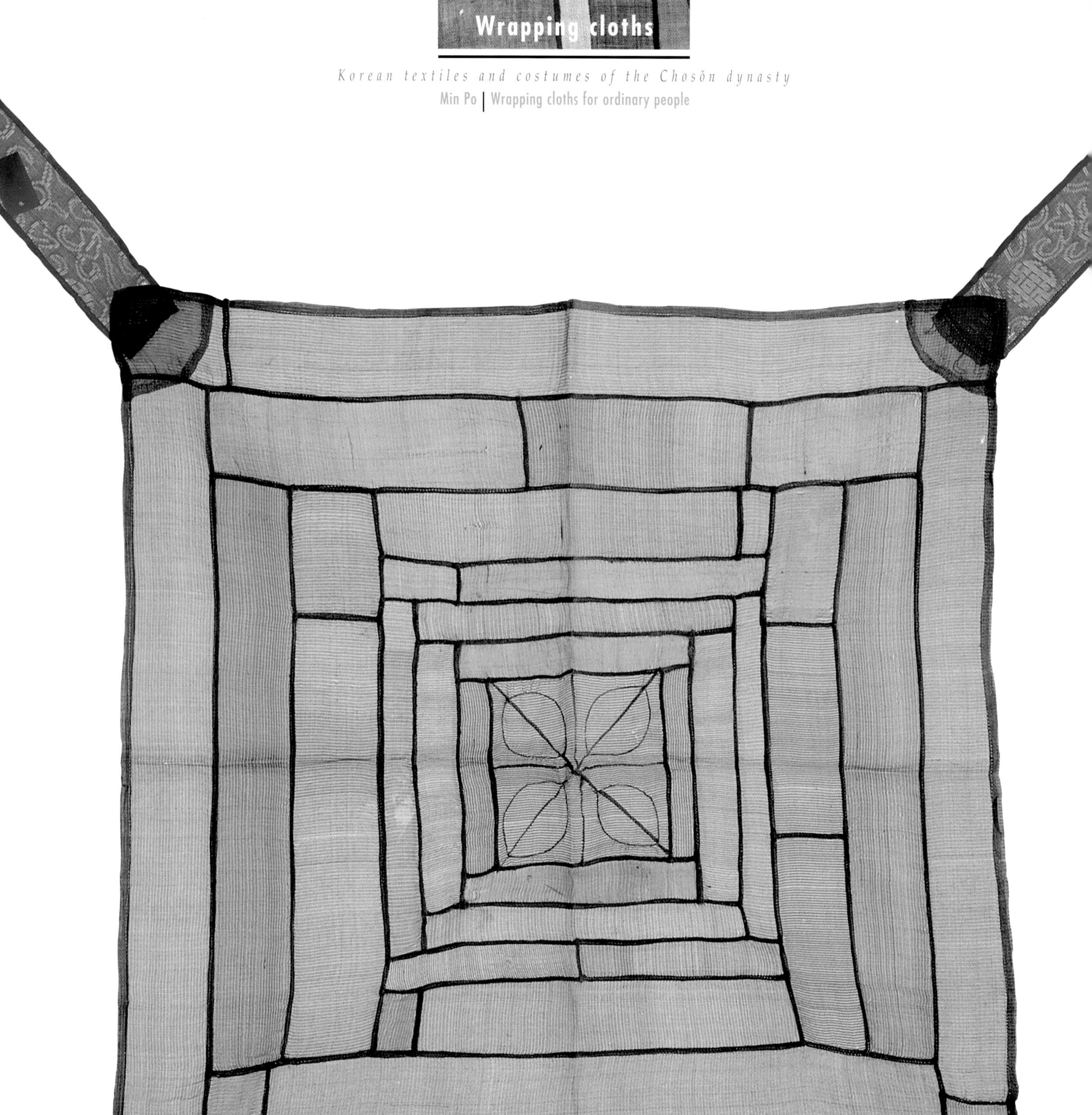

28. Oppo, thin silk *(sa)* with patchwork design, 19th century, (50cm, 50cm).

29. Oppo, thin silk *(sa)* with patchwork design, 19th century, (95cm, 95cm).

30. Oppo, self - patterned silk *(sa)* with patchwork design, 19th century, (95cm, 95cm).

31. **Pach'im Po** (wrapping cloth to cover a tray or table), ramie *(moshi)* with patchwork design, red, 18th century, (67cm, 52cm).

32. Oppo, ramie *(moshi)* with patchwork design, 19th century, (127cm, 133cm).

33. Ch'ŏn Po (wrapping cloth for fabrics), ramie *(moshi)* with patchwork design, 19th centuury, (58cm, 57cm).

34. Ch'ŏn Po, ramie *(moshi)* with patchwork design, 19th century,(41cm, 41cm).

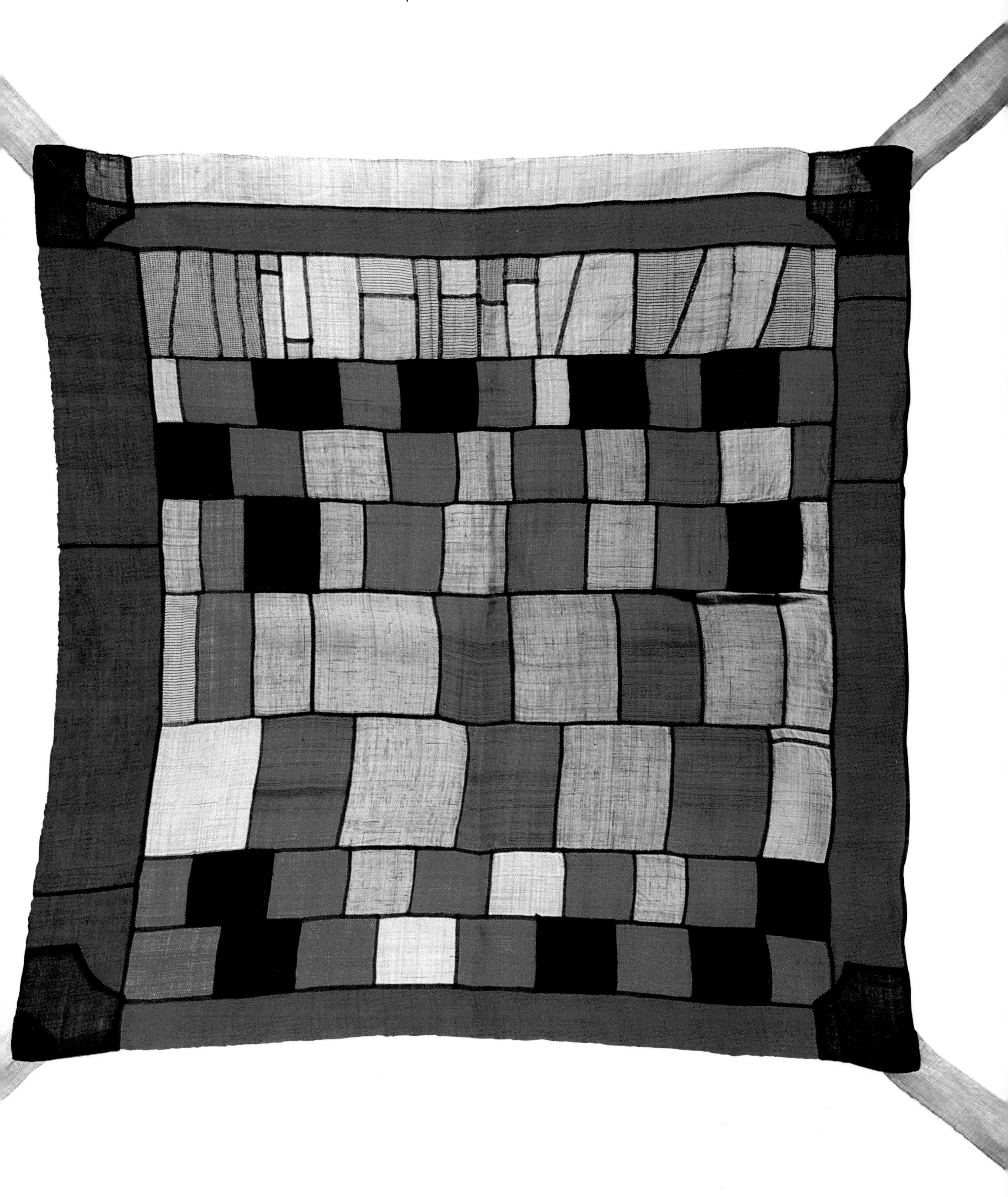

35. Oppo, ramie *(moshi)* with patchwork design, 19th century (58cm, 59cm).

36. Oppo, ramie *(moshi)* with patchwork design, 19th century, (82cm, 86cm).

37. Yibul Po (wrapping cloth for bedding), linen *(pe)* and hemp *(sambe)* with patchwork design, blue, 18th century, (145cm, 145cm).

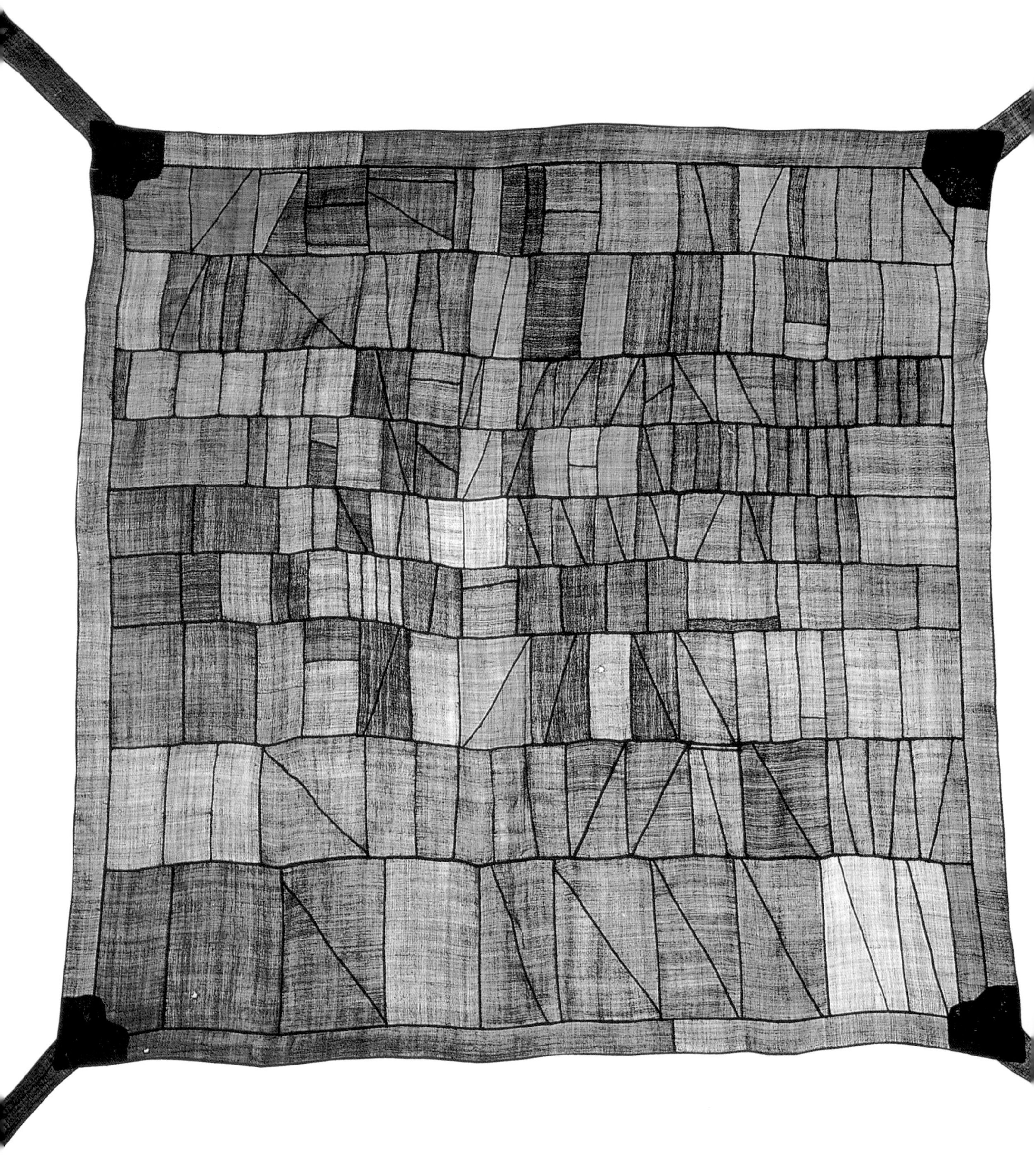

38.Yibul Po, linen *(pe)* and hemp *(sambe)* with patchwork design, black, 18th century, (165cm, 165cm).

39. Sang Po (wrapping cloth for covering a table or tray), self - patterned silk *(sa)* with cintamani design, 19th century, (39cm, 39cm).

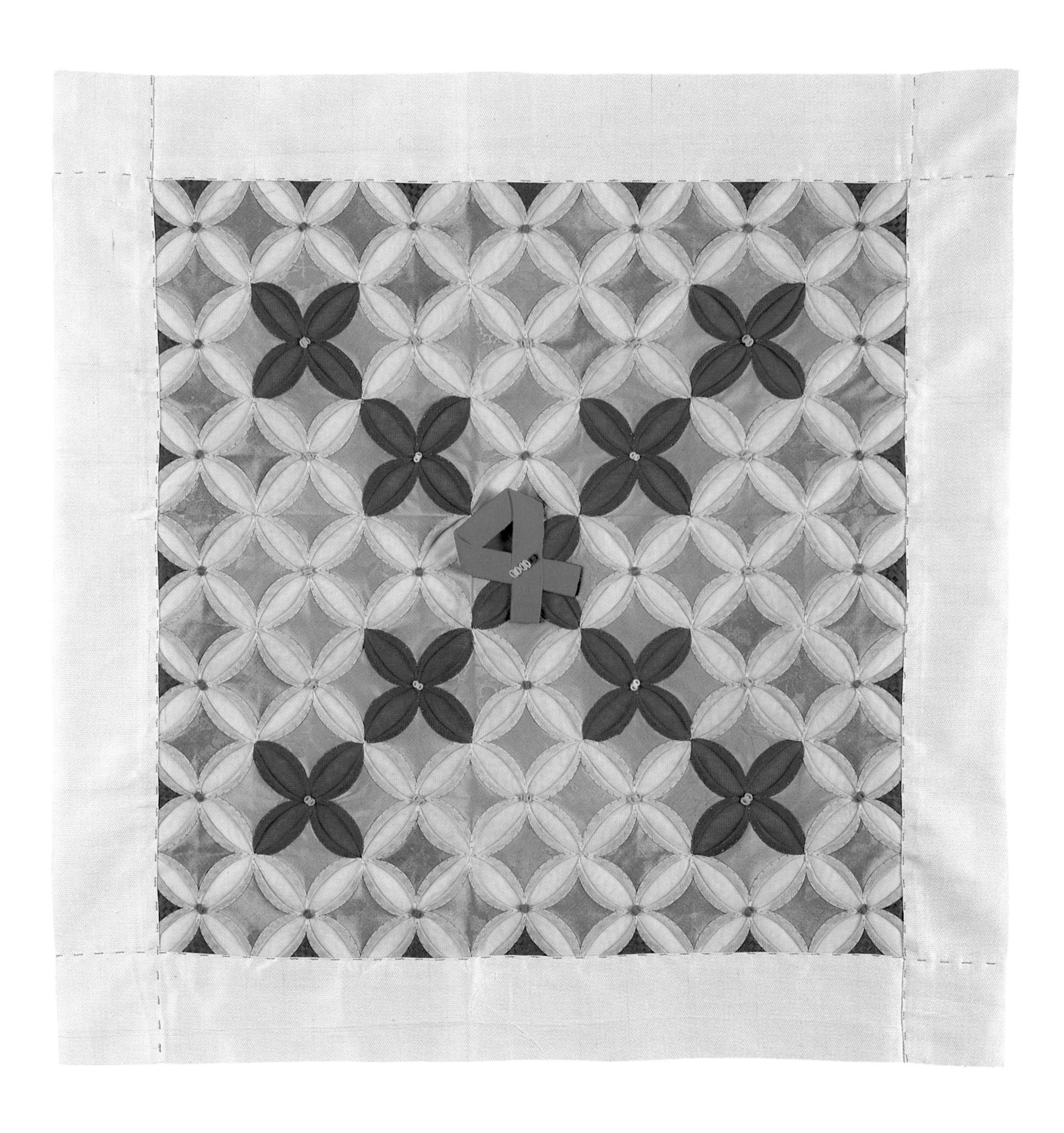

40. Sang Po, self-patterned silk *(sa)* with cintamani design, 19th century, (55cm, 55cm).

41. Pach'im Po, self-patterned silk *(sa)* with patchwork design, 19th century, (49cm, 49cm).

42. Norigae Po (wrapping cloth for small personal ornaments), satin weave silk *(tan)* with patchwork design, 19th century, (41cm, 41cm).

43. Yedan Po (wrapping cloth for gifts by the bride's family to the groom's family), satin weave silk *(tan)* with patchwork design and central embroidered square, 19th century, (56cm, 56cm).

44. Yedan Po, satin weave silk with patchwork design and border *(tan, hangna and myŏngju)*, 19th century, (67cm, 67cm).

45. **Sikji Po** (oiled paper wrapping cloth), oiled paper with cut - out paper patterns of flowers, bats and butterflies, 19th century, (53cm, 41.5cm).

46. Norigae Po (wrapping cloth for small personal ornaments), cotton *(myŏn)* with embroidered design of flower and butterfly in one corner, 19th century, (31cm, 31cm).

47. Oppo (wrapping cloth for clothing), ramie *(moshi)* with embroidered floral design in the corners, 19th century, (66cm, 66cm).

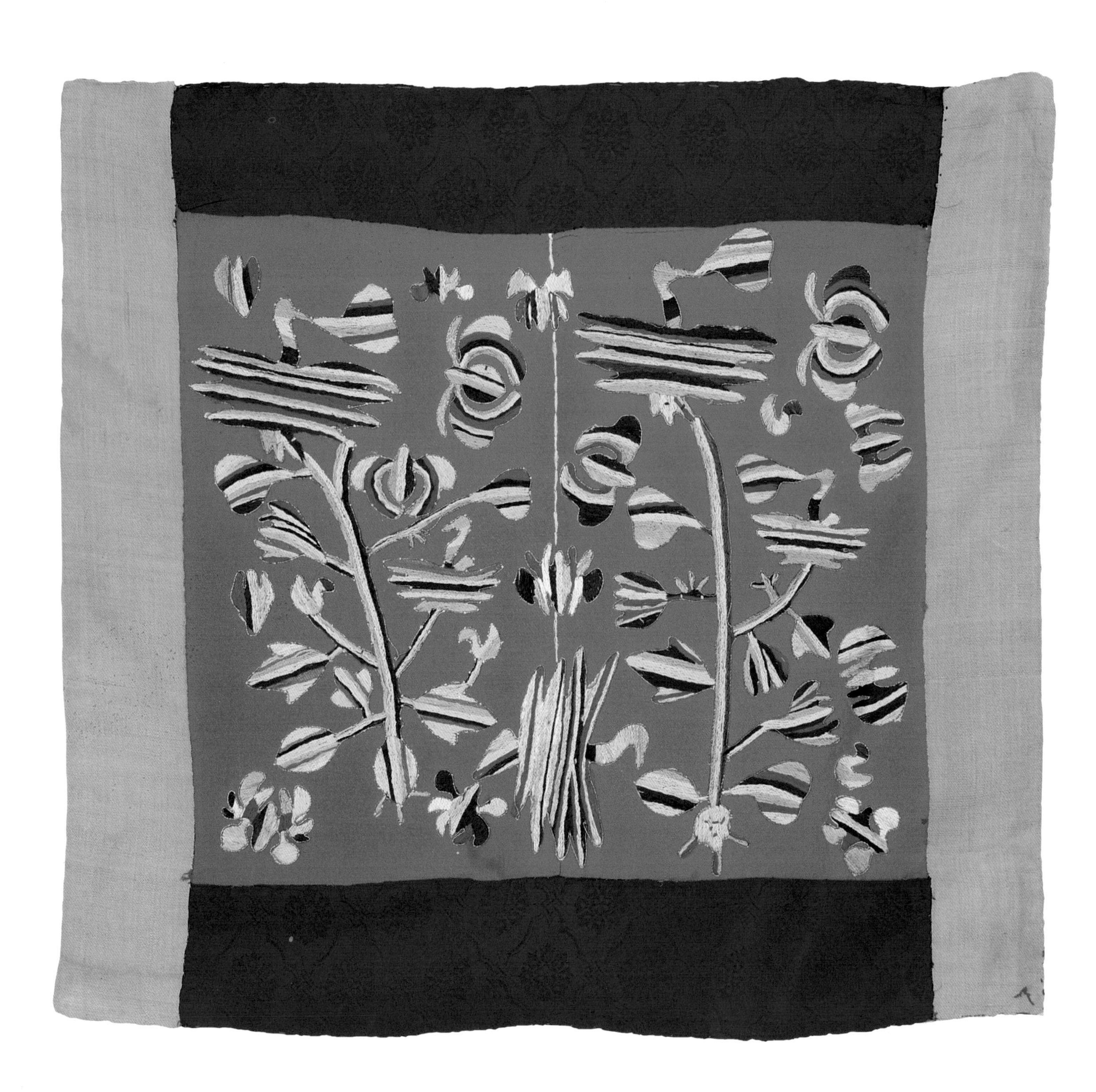

48. Yemul Po (wrapping cloth for gifts from the groom's parents to the bride and also for gifts exchanged by the bride and the groom), silk *(tan and myŏngju)* with embroidered design of pomegranate trees, butterflies and cranes, 19th century, (39cm, 36cm).

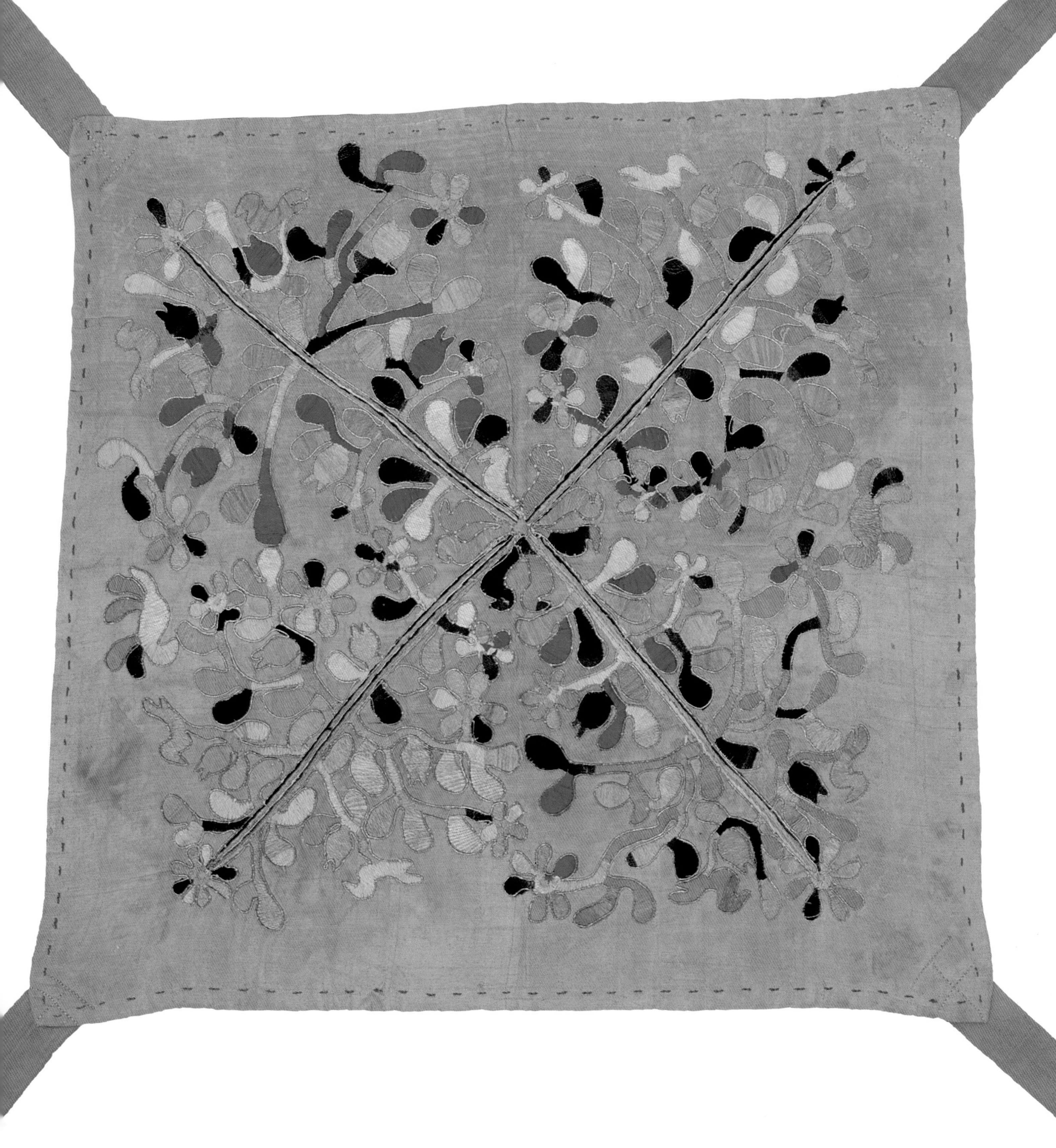

49. Kirŏgi Po (wrapping cloth for a goose for the traditional wedding ceremony), silk *(myŏngju)* with embroidered design of tree, birds, flowers and pomegranates, 19th century, (30cm, 30cm).

50. Yemul Po, cotton *(myŏn)* with embroidered design of pomegranate tree, cranes and other birds, butterflies and characters for happiness, 19th century, (38cm, 38cm).

51.Yemul Po, cotton *(myŏn)* with embroidered design of pomegranate tree, butterflies, phoenix and other birds, 19th century, (42cm, 40cm).

52. Yemul Po, cotton *(myŏn)* with embroidered design of pomegranate tree, birds, and butterflies, 19th century, (41cm, 42cm)

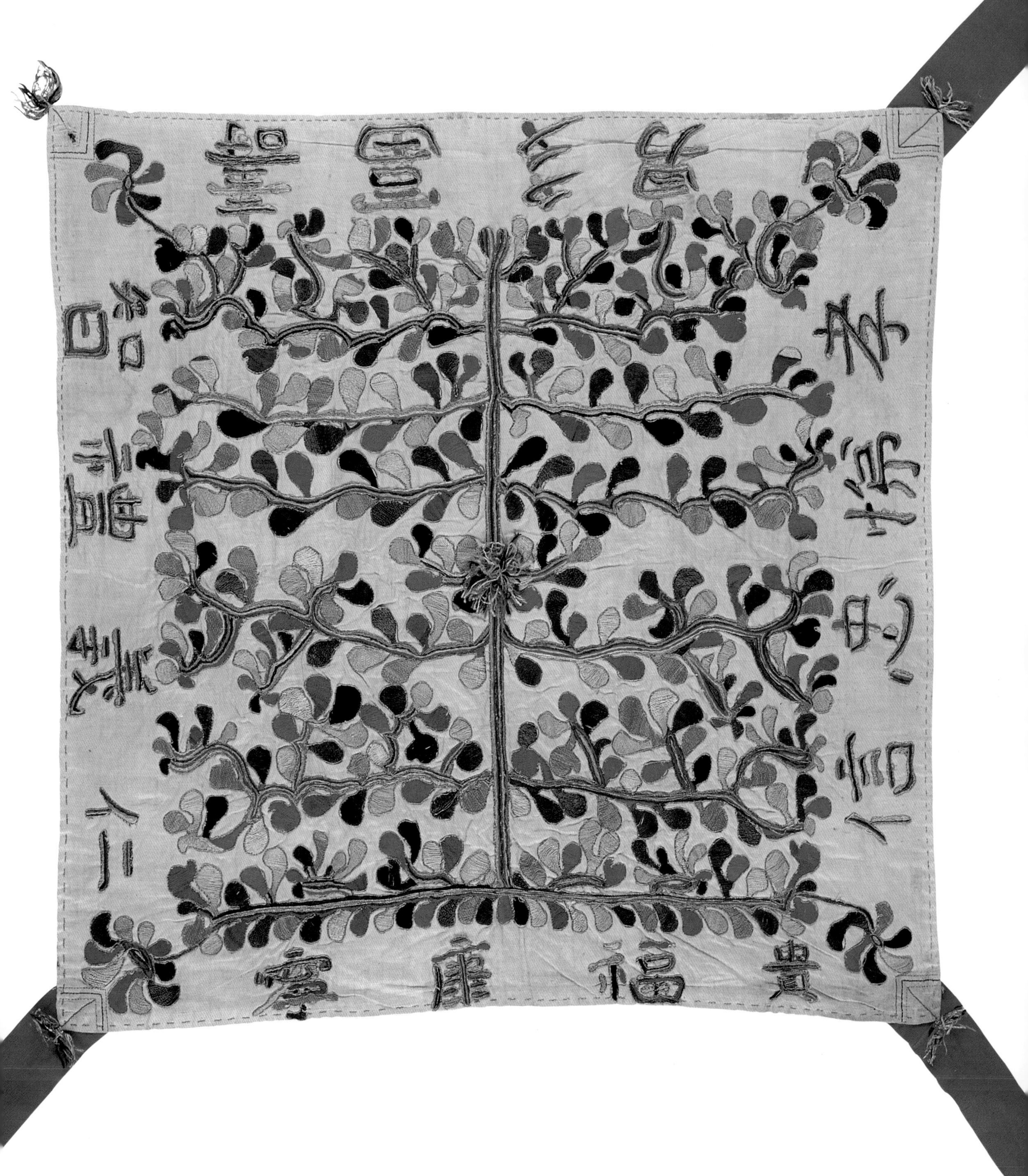

53. Kirŏgi Po, cotton *(myŏn)* with embroidered design of tree, birds and character border, 19th century, (44cm, 44cm).

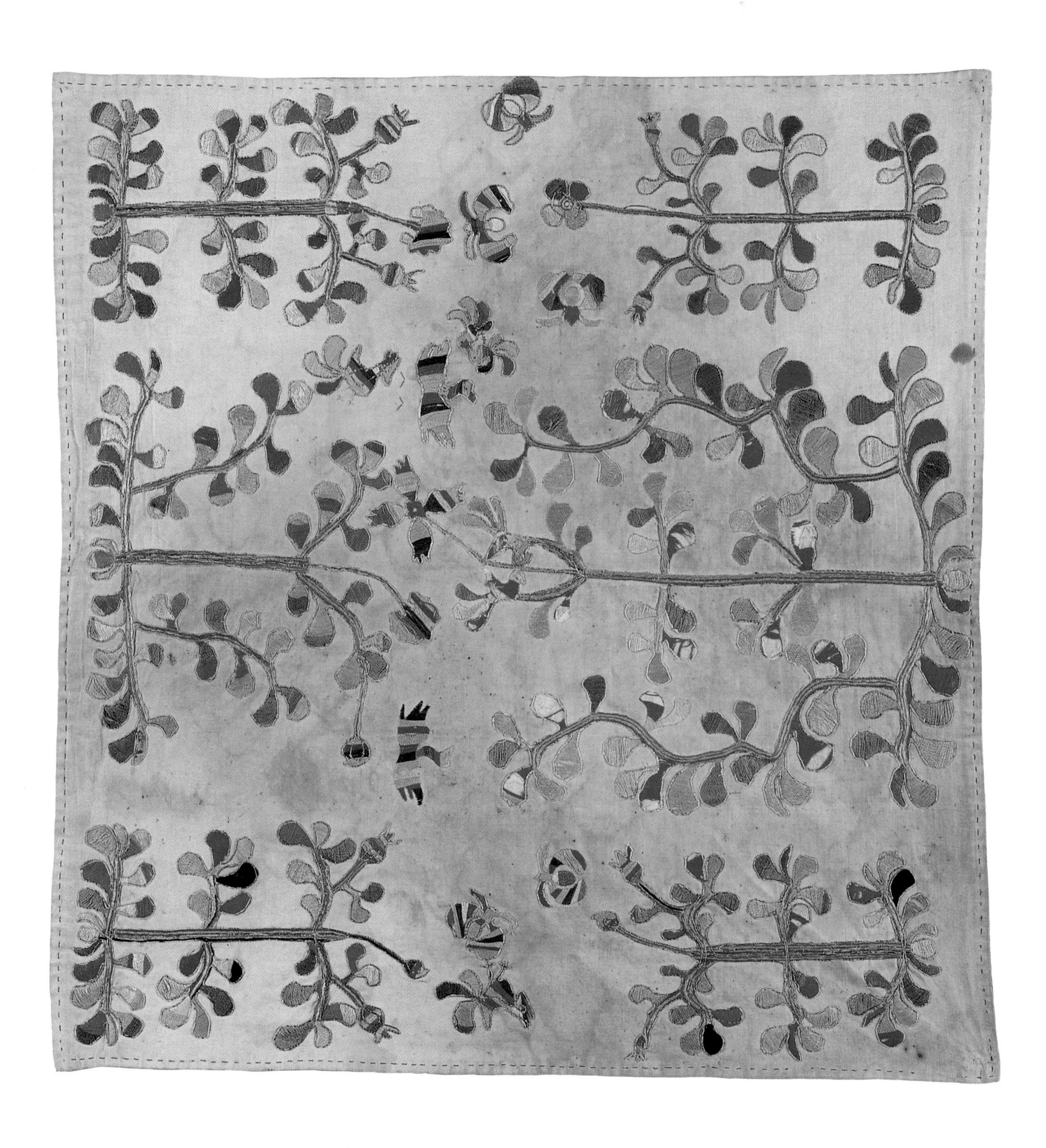

54. Yemul Po, cotton *(myŏn)* with embroidered design of pomegranate tree, cranes and other birds and butterflies, 19th century, (48cm, 45cm).

55. Yemul Po, cotton *(myŏn)* with embroidered design of flowering tree, 19th century, (41cm, 41cm).

56. Yemul Po, cotton *(myŏn)* with embroidered floral design, 19th century, (36cm, 36.5cm).

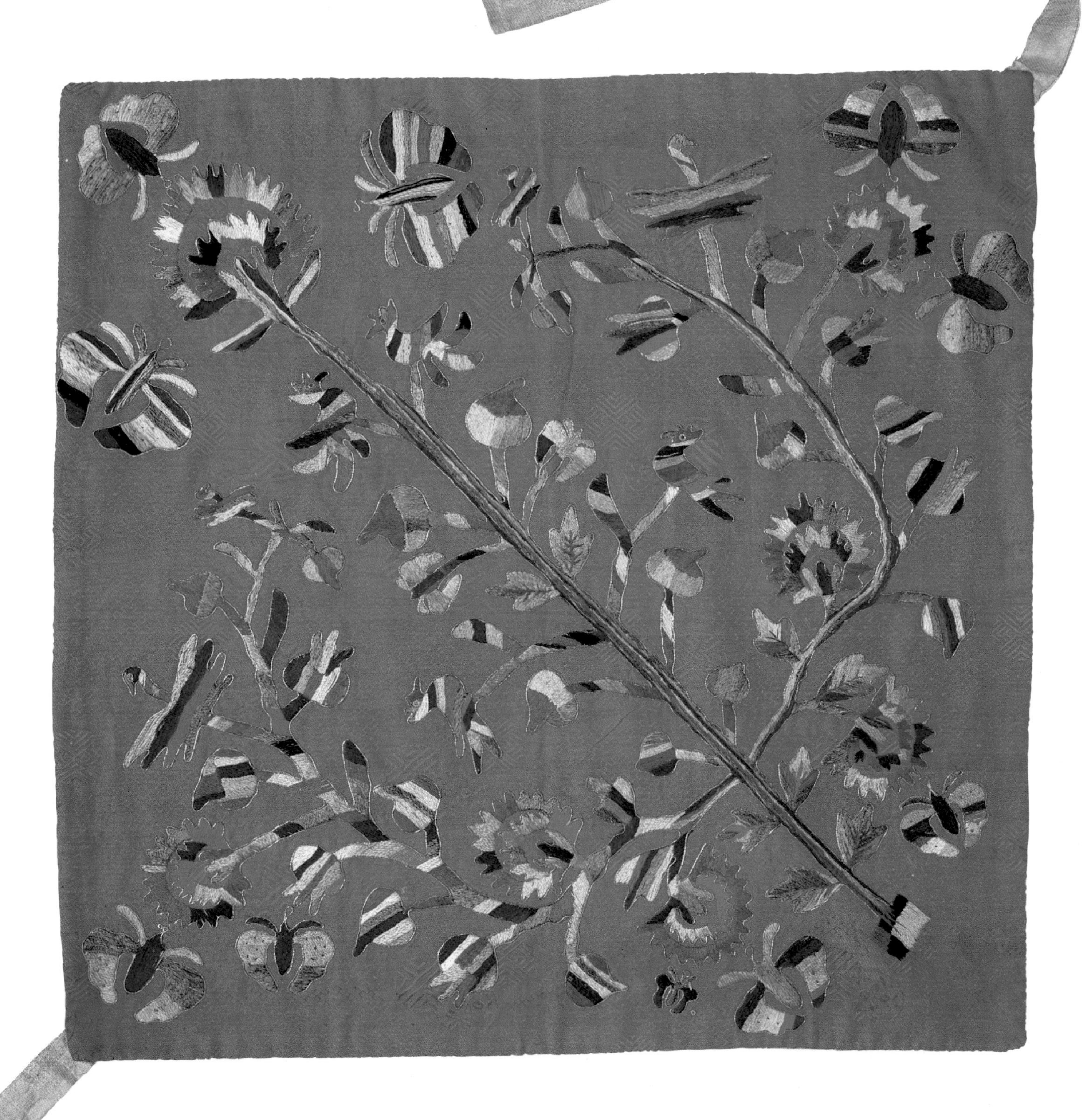

57. Kirŏgi Po, self-patterned silk *(tan)* with embroidered design of pomegranate tree, fruits, flowers and cranes, 19th century, (44cm, 44cm).

58. Yibul Po (wrapping cloth for bedding), line - patterned silk gauze *(sa)* decorated with patchwork design, 19th century, (112cm, 112cm).

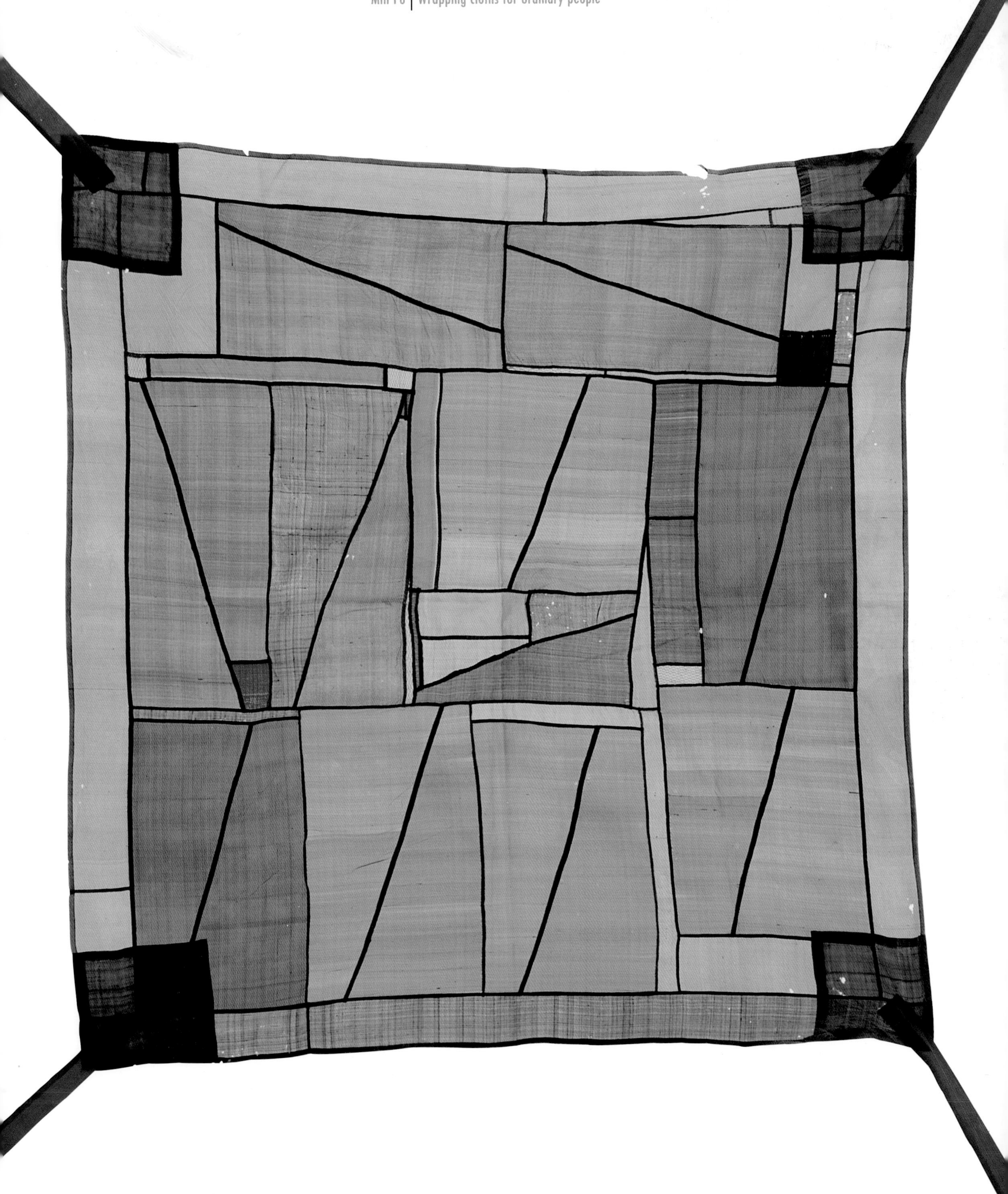

59. Oppo, unpatterned and self - patterned silk *(myŏngju and sa)* decorated with patchwork design, 19th century, (74cm, 75cm).

60. Oppo, silk *(myŏngju)* decorated with patchwork design, 19th century, (85cm, 85cm).

61. Oppo, unpatterned and self - patterned silk *(myŏngju and sa)* with patchwork design, 19th century, (59cm, 59cm).

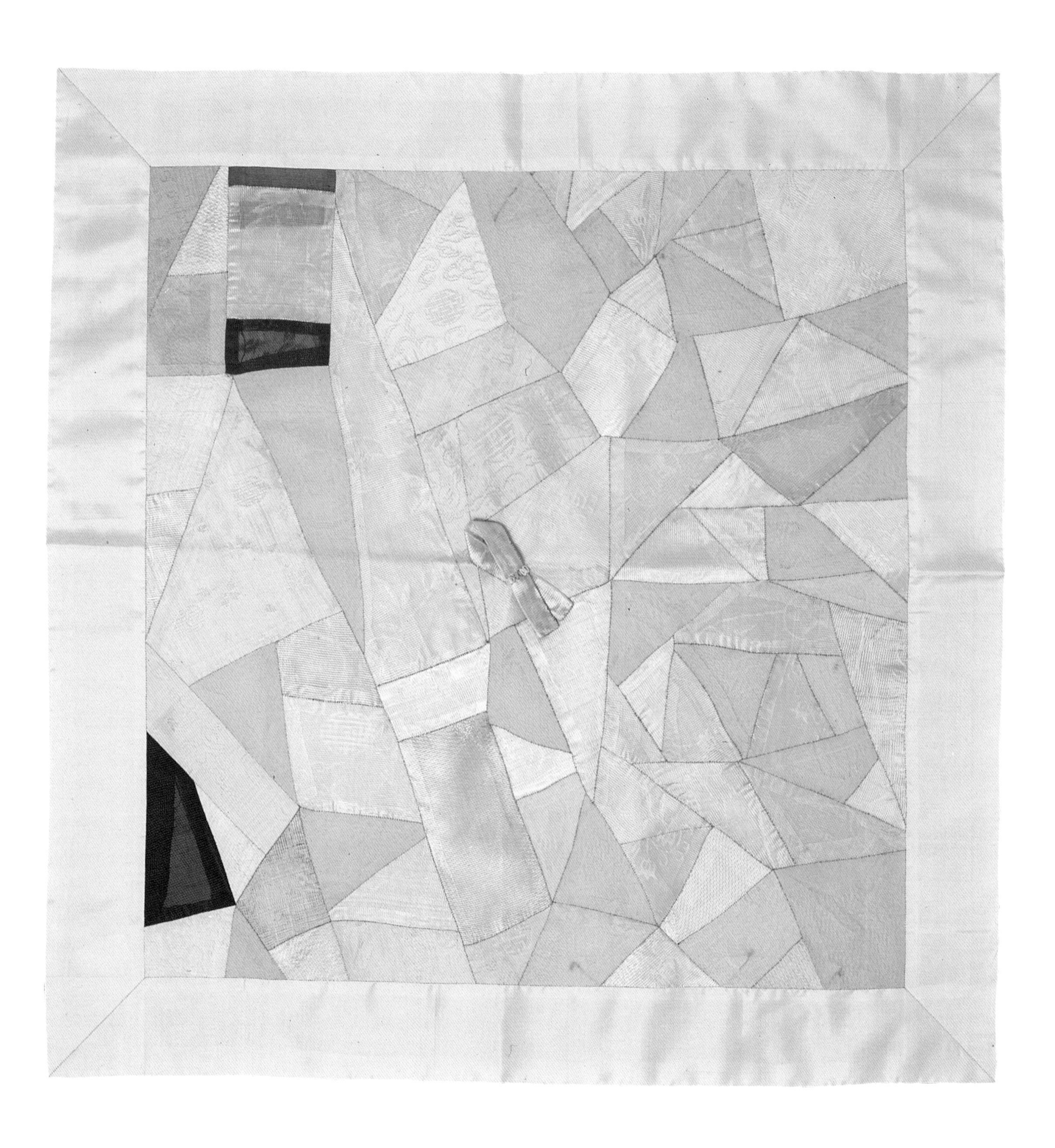

62. Sang Po, self - patterned silk *(sa)* with patchwork design, 19th century, (56cm, 56.5cm).

63. Oppo, cotton *(myŏn)* decorated with patchwork design, 19th century, (52cm, 52cm)

List of illustrated objects

Costume

1. Wŏnsam (bridal robe), silk (*tan*) with self-patterned design; green, red, blue, yellow, pink, and white, 19th century, (220cm, 122cm).

2. Hwarrot (bridal robe), silk (*tan*) embroidered with floral, bird and character design; red, blue, yellow, pink, and white, 18th century, (113cm, 146cm).

3. Tang'ui (woman's jacket), silk (*tan*) with self-patterned peony design; green, white and red, 19th century, (134cm, 84cm).

4. Ch'ima (skirt), silk (*sa*) with self-patterned design, red, 19th century, (114cm, 112cm).

5. Chŏgori (woman's jacket), silk (*sa*) with self-patterned design, yellow and red, 19th century, (26cm, 130cm).

6. a-b Paeja chŏgori (man's jacket and vest), 19th century,
a. Paeja (vest) - silk (*sa*) with self-patterned design, green, (62cm, 93cm).
b. Chŏgori (jacket) - silk (*myŏngju*), purple, (61cm, 58cm).

7. Paeja (baby's vest), silk (*sa*) with self-patterned design, red, blue, yellow, and black, 19th century, (27cm, 34cm).

8. a-b. Mubok (shaman's robe and long vest), 19th century
a. Robe - silk (*sa*), green and red, (129cm, 147cm).
b. Long vest - silk (*sa*), black, (220cm, 122cm).

9. a-d. Chobok (Confucian scholar's ceremonial robe), 19th century
a. Chŏkch'oui (red coat), silk (*sa*), (188cm, 116cm).
b. Ch'ŏng ch'oui (blue coat), silk (*sa*), (146cm, 180cm).
c. Hunsang (apron), silk, red, (97cm, 88cm).
d. Husu (insignia), silk embroidered with cranes, lotus scrolls, clouds and swastika designs, (11cm, 31.5cm).

Wrapping cloths

Kung po (wrapping cloths for the Palace)

10. Princess Myong'an's Yedan Po (wrapping cloth for gifts by the bride's family to the groom's family), silk (*tan*) with seven treasures and cloud pattern, blue, 17th century, (107cm, 111cm).

11. Queen's Su Po (embroidered wrapping cloth), silk (tan) embroidered with bird and flower design, 17th century, (82cm, 93cm).

12. Yedan Su Po (wrapping cloth for gift for wedding ceremony), silk (*tan*) embroidered with floral decoration, 18th century, (49cm, 49cm).

13. Kŭmbak Po (wrapping cloth with gold design), silk (*tan*) with pressed gold design, red, 19th century, (72cm, 72cm).

14. Tangch'ae Po (wrapping cloth with painted design), ramie (*moshi*) painted with confronting phoenixes, floral and other auspicious patterns in red and blue colours, 19th century (70cm, 70cm).

15. Tangch'ae Po (wrapping cloth with painted design), cotton (*myŏn*) painted with auspicious symbols of peonies, cranes, turtles, phoenix and deer, 19th century, (93cm, 93cm).

16. Tangch'ae Po (wrapping cloth with painted design), cotton (*myŏn*) painted with floral and designs, 19th century, (93cm, 97cm).

Min Po (wrapping cloths for ordinary people)

A) Chogak Po (wrapping cloths with patchwork designs-regular)

17. Sang Po (wrapping cloth for covering a food table or tray), silk (*sa*) with self-patterned design, unlined, 19th century, 52cm, 52cm).

18. Sang Po, silk (*sa*) with self-patterned design, 19th century, (44cm, 44cm).

19. Sang Po, silk (*sa*) with self-patterned design, 19th century, (38cm, 38cm).

20. Sang Po, self-patterned and unpatterned silk (*sa* and *myŏngju*), 19th century, (42cm, 42cm).

21. Yuji Sang Po (wrapping cloth lined with oiled paper for covering food), self-patterned silk (*sa*) with patchwork design and lined with oil paper (*yuji*), 19th century, (49.5cm, 49cm).

22. Sang Po, silk (*sa*) with self-patterned design, 19th century, (48cm, 48cm).

23. Sang Po, silk (*sa*) with self-patterned design, 19th century, (51cm, 50cm).

24. Sang Po, silk (*sa*) with self-patterned design, 19th century, (47cm, 46cm).

25. Sang Po, silk (*sa)* with self-patterned design, 19th century, (48cm, 48cm).

B) Ramie, linen, hemp and thin silk wrapping cloths

26. Oppo (wrapping cloth for clothing), ramie (*moshi*) with patchwork design, 19th century, (45cm, 45cm).

27. Oppo, ramie (*moshi*) with patchwork design, 19th century, (45cm, 45cm).

28. Oppo, thin silk (*sa*) with patchwork design, 19th century, (50cm, 50cm).

29. Oppo, thin silk (*sa*) with patchwork design, 19th century, (95cm, 95cm).

30. Oppo, self-patterned silk (*sa*) with patchwork design, 19th century, (95cm, 95cm).

31. Pach'im Po (wrapping cloth to cover a tray or table), ramie (*moshi*) with patchwork design, red, 18th century, (67cm, 52cm).

32. Oppo, ramie (*moshi*) with patchwork design, 19th century, (127cm, 133cm).

33. Ch'ŏn Po (wrapping cloth for fabrics), ramie (*moshi*) with patchwork design, 19th centuury, (58cm, 57cm).

34. Ch'ŏn Po, ramie (*moshi*) with patchwork design, 19th century, (41cm, 41cm).

35. Oppo, ramie (*moshi*) with patchwork design, 19th century (58cm, 59cm).

36. Oppo, ramie (*moshi*) with patchwork design, 19th century, (82cm, 86cm).

37. Yibul Po (wrapping cloth for bedding), linen (*pe*) and hemp (*sambe*) with patchwork design, blue, 18th century, (145cm 145cm).

38. Yibul Po, linen (*pe*) and hemp (*sambe*) with patchwork design, black, 18th century, (165cm, 165cm).

C) Chogak Po (Wrapping cloths with patchwork design-and Sikji Po (Oiled paper wrapping cloths) - cut-out paper design

39. Sang Po (wrapping cloth for covering a table or tray), self-patterned silk (*sa*) with cintamani design, 19th century, (39cm, 39cm).

40. Sang Po, self-patterned silk (*sa*) with cintamani design, 19th century, (55cm, 55cm).

41. Pach'im Po, self-patterned silk (*sa*) with patchwork design, 19th century, (49cm, 49cm).

42. Norigae Po (wrapping cloth for small personal ornaments), satin weave silk (*tan*) with patchwork design, 19th century, (41cm, 41cm).

43. Yedan Po (wrapping cloth for gifts by the bride's family to the groom's family), satin weave silk (*tan*) with patchwork design and central embroidered square, 19th century, (56cm, 56cm).

44. Yedan Po, satin weave silk with patchwork design and border (*tan, hangna* and *myŏngju*), 19th century, (67cm, 67cm).

45. Sikji Po (oiled paper wrapping cloth), oiled paper with cut-out paper patterns of flowers, bats and butterflies,19th century, (53cm, 41.5cm).

D) Su Po (Wrapping Cloths with embroidered design)

46. Norigae Po (wrapping cloth for small personal ornaments), cotton (*myŏn*) with embroidered design of flower and butterfly in one corner, 19th century, (31cm, 31cm).

47. Oppo (wrapping cloth for clothing), ramie (*moshi*) with embroidered floral design in the corners, 19th century, (66cm, 66cm).

48. Yemul Po (wrapping cloth for gifts from the groom's parents to the bride and also for gifts exchanged by the bride and the groom), silk (*tan* and *myŏngju*) with embroidered design of pomegranate trees, butterflies, and cranes,19th century, (39cm, 36cm).

49. Kirŏgi Po (wrapping cloth for a goose for the traditional wedding ceremony), silk (*myŏngju*) with embroidered design of tree, birds, flowers and pomegranates, 19th century, (30cm, 30cm).

50. Yemul Po, cotton (*myŏn*) with embroidered design of pomegranate tree, cranes and other birds, butterflies, and characters for happiness, 19th century, (38cm, 38cm).

51.Yemul Po, cotton (*myŏn*) with embroidered design of pomegranate tree, butterflies, phoenix and other birds, 19th century, (42cm, 40cm).

52. Yemul Po, cotton (*myŏn*) with embroidered design of pomegranate tree, birds, and butterflies, 19th century, (41cm, 42cm).

53. Kirŏgi Po, cotton (*myŏn*) with embroidered design of tree, birds and character border, 19th century, (44cm, 44cm).

54. Yemul Po, cotton (*myŏn*) with embroidered design of pomegranate tree, cranes and other birds and butterflies, 19th century, (48cm, 45cm).

55. Yemul Po, cotton (*myŏn*) with embroidered design of flowering tree, 19th century, (41cm, 41cm).

56. Yemul Po, cotton (*myŏn*) with embroidered floral design, 19th century, (36cm, 36.5cm).

57. Kirŏgi Po, self-patterned silk (*tan*) with embroidered design of pomegranate tree, fruits, flowers and cranes, 19th century, (44cm, 44cm).

E) Abstract patchwork design

58. Yibul Po (wrapping cloth for bedding), line-patterned silk gauze (*sa*) decorated with patchwork design, 19th century, (112cm, 112cm).

59. Oppo, unpatterned and self-patterned silk (*myŏngju* and *sa*) decorated with patchwork design, 19th century, (74cm, 75cm).

60. Oppo, silk (*myŏngju*) decorated with patchwork design, 19th century, (85cm, 85cm).

61. Oppo, unpatterned and self-patterned silk (*myŏngju* and *sa*) with patchwork design, 19th century, (59cm, 59cm).

62. Sang Po, self-patterned silk (*sa*) with patchwork design, 19th century, (56cm, 56.5cm).

63. Oppo, cotton (*myŏn*) decorated with patchwork design, 19th century, (52cm, 52cm).

Selected bibliography

Choe-wall, Yang-hi, trans. *Memoirs of a Korean queen, Lady Hong*, KPI, London & New York, 1985.

Han'guk ui Mi. (Beauty of Korea: traditional costume, ornaments and wrapping cloths), exhibition catalogue, National Museum of Korea, Seoul, 1988.

Han Yŏnghwa, *Chŏn'tong Chasu* (Traditional embroidery), Taewŏn-sa, Seoul, 1989.

Huh Dong-hwa. *Crafts of the inner court*, The Museum of Korean Embroidery, Seoul, 1987.

Huh Dong-hwa. *The wonder cloth*, The Museum of Korean Embroidery, Seoul, 1988.

Huh Dong-hwa. *Yet Chogak Po Chŏn.* (Exhibition of traditional patchwork wrapping cloths), exhibition catalogue, Taejŏn Expo, 7 August - 7 November, 1993.

Huh Dong-hwa and Kumja Paik Kim, *Profusion of colour: Korean costumes and wrapping cloths of the Chosŏn dynasty*, exhibition catalogue, The Asian Art Museum of San Francisco and The Museum of Korean Embroidery, Seoul, 28 February - 30 April, 1995.

Kim, Yongsuk. *Han'guk yŏsoska* (History of customs and manners of Korean women), Minŭmsa, Seoul, 1989.
Lee, Ki-baik. A *new history of Korea*, trans by Edward W Wagner with Edward J Schultz, Harvard University Press, Cambridge, Massachusetts, 1984.

Lee, Peter H. *Anthology of Korean literature*, The University Press of Hawaii, Honolulu, 1981.

Lee, Peter H. *Sourcebook of Korean civilisation*, vol 1, Columbia University Press, New York, 1993.

Middleton, Sheila Hoey, *Traditional Korean wrapping cloths*, exhibition catalogue, Fitzwilliam Museum, Cambridge, 13 March - 29 April, 1990 ; Ashmolean Museum, Oxford, 9 May - 1 July, 1990.

Yi, Sŏng-mi. *Korean costumes and textiles*, exhibition catalogue, IBM Gallery of Science and Art, New York, 14 April - 13 June, 1992.